THE SYRIAN GODDESS, ON COINS OF HIERAPOLIS

Cf. Figs. 5, 7   *See p.* 15

Lucian's
On The Syrian Goddess
A Dual Language Edition

English Translation (1913) by
Herbert A. Strong, M.A. LL.D.

with Notes and Introduction (1913) by
John Garstang, M.A. D.Sc.

Greek Text Edited (1921) by
A. M. Harmon

Edited by
Evan Hayes and Stephen Nimis

Faenum Publishing
Oxford, Ohio

Lucian's On the Syrian Goddess: *A Dual Language Edition*

First Edition

© 2013 by Evan Hayes and Stephen Nimis

All rights reserved. Subject to the exception immediately following, this book may not be reproduced, in whole or in part, in any form (beyond copying permitted by Sections 107 and 108 of the U.S. Copyright Law and except by reviewers for the public press), without written permission from the publisher.

The authors have made a version of this work available (via email) under a Creative Commons Attribution-Noncommercial-Share Alike 3.0 License. The terms of the license can be accessed at creativecommons.org.

Accordingly, you are free to copy, alter and distribute this work under the following conditions:
   You must attribute the work to the author (but not in a way that suggests that the author endorses your alterations to the work).
   You may not use this work for commercial purposes.
   If you alter, transform or build up this work, you may distribute the resulting work only under the same or similar license as this one.

Unless otherwise noted, all images appearing in this edition are in the public domain.

ISBN: 978-0-9832228-6-6

Published by Faenum Publishing, Ltd.
Cover Design: Evan Hayes

SUMMARY OF CONTENTS

Editors' Note vii
List of Illustrations xi
Introduction—The Syrian Goddess in History and Art . . 1
Life of Lucian 25
Lucian's Text: Analysis of Subject-Matter 33
Greek Text and English Translation 36
Appendix—Descriptions of the Site of Hierapolis Syriae,
   the Sacred City, by Maundrell, Pocock,
   and Chesney. 97
Bibliography 103
Index 105

EDITORS' NOTE

This book presents the Greek text of Lucian's *De dea Syria* with a facing English translation. The Greek text is that of A. M. Harmon, from the Loeb Classical Library, which is in the public domain and available as a pdf. This text has also been digitized by the Perseus Project (perseus.tufts.edu). Because the Greek is Ionic and a pastiche of Herodotus, Harmon chose to link his text to a translation in the style of Sir John Mandeville, which is quaint and interesting, but not particularly helpful to someone trying to understand the Greek. Meanwhile, the idiomatic translation of Herbert A. Strong from 1912 is also in the public domain and is available online at the Internet Sacred Texts Archive (sacred-texts.com), so we have reset both texts, making a number of very minor corrections, and placed them on opposing pages. We have also included the original introduction by John Garstang, the extensive footnotes to the text that were included in the translation, and the life of Lucian by H. A. Strong included there. The text in this format will be useful to those wishing to read the English translation while looking at the Greek version, or vice versa. We refer those interested in reading the Greek with grammatical and lexical assistance to our intermediate Greek reader, cited below.

We have also included the bibliography cited by Strong, although much has been written about this text in the last hundred years. Of this additional bibliography, we cite the following examples:

Editions, Translations and Commentaries

Attridge, H. W. and R. A. Ogden, tr. *The Syrian Goddess (De dea Syria) attributed to Lucian.* Scholars Press: Missoula, MT. 1979.

Bompaire, J. Lucien: *Oevres*. Budé: Paris, 1993. Vol. 1

Hayes, E. and Stephen Nimis. *Lucian's On the Syrian Goddess*: An Intermediate Greek Reader: Greek Text with Running Vocabulary and Commentary. Faenum Ltd.; Oxford, OH, 2012.

Lightfoot, J. L. *Lucian On the Syrian Goddess: Text Translation and Commentary*. Oxford UP: Oxford, 2003.

Macleod, M. D. *Lucian, Opera*. Oxford Classical Texts, Oxford, 1972.

Meunier, Mario. *La Déesse syrienne: traduction nouvelle avec prolégomènes et notes*. Editions Janick, Paris: 1947.

Critical studies

Dirven, L. "The Author of the *De Dea Syria* and his Cultural Heritage." *Numen* 44 (1997), 153-97.

Elsner, J. "Describing Self in the Language of the Other: Pseudo(?) Lucian at the Temple of Hierapolis," in S. Goldhill (ed) *Being Greek under Rome: Cultural Identity, the Second Sophistic and the Development of Empire* (Cambridge, 2001), 123-53.

Hörig, M. "Dea Syria-Atargatis." *Aufstieg und Niedergang der römische Welt* II 17.3 (1984), 1536-81.

Oden, R. A., Jr. *Studies in Lucian's De Syria dea*. Missoula, Mont.: Scholars Press, 1977.

LIST OF ILLUSTRATIONS

Plate.   The Syrian Goddess, etc., on Coins
         of Hierapolis . . . . *Frontispiece*

Fig. 1. The Hittite "Hadad" at Malâtia. 4

Fig. 2. The Chief Hittite God and Goddess
         at Boghaz-Keui 5

Fig. 3. The Hittite Bull-God at Eyuk. 7

Fig. 4. The Hittite Draped Altar-Pedestal
         at Fraktin. 18

Fig. 5. Atargatis and Her Priest, b.c. 332.
         (From a Coin) 20

Fig. 6. Temple of Byblos. (From a Coin) 29

Fig. 7. The God and Goddess of Hierapolis.
         (From a Coin) 72

Fig. 8. The Phrygian Goddess (Kybele) in the West.
         (From a Roman Lamp) 73

INTRODUCTION
The Syrian Goddess In History And Art

THE dawn of history in all parts of Western Asia discloses the established worship of a nature-goddess in whom the productive powers of the earth were personified.[1] She is our Mother Earth, known otherwise as the Mother Goddess or Great Mother. Among the Babylonians[2] and northern Semites she was called Ishtar: she is the Ashtoreth of the Bible, and the Astarte of Phœnicia. In Syria her name was 'Athar, and in Cilicia it had the form of 'Ate ('Atheh). At Hierapolis, with which we are primarily concerned, it appears in later Aramaic as Atargatis, a compound of the Syrian and Cilician forms.[3] In Asia Minor, where the influence of the Semitic language did not prevail, her various names have not survived, though it is recorded by a later Greek writer as "Ma" at one of her mountain shrines, and as Agdistis amongst one tribe of the Phrygians[4] and probably at Pessinus. These differences, however, are partly questions of local tongue; for in one way and another there was still a prevailing similarity between the

---

1. We do not wish to imply a necessarily common "origin" or real identity in the various local aspects of this divinity.
2. Among the pre-Semitic population she appears as *Nanai*. *Cf.* Ed. Meyer in Roscher's *Lexikon*—ASTARTE.
3. See n. 57, p. 16, and n. 25, p. 7. *Cf.* Frazer, *Adonis, Attis, and Osiris*, p. 130, n. 1; Ed. Meyer, *Gesch. des Alth.*, i. (1st edn.), p. 247, § 205.
4. Strabo, x. iii. 12; xii. ii. 3.

The probable mention of "Astarte of the Land of the Hittites," as the leading Hittite goddess among the witnesses to the treaty with Egypt (c. B.C. 1271), must be assumed at present to refer to Northern Syria. The allusion is none the less significant, implying an identification of the Hittite deity with Ishtar. This rendering of the Egyptian text is due to an emendation suggested by Müller (*Vorderas. Ges.* VII., 5), and accepted as probable by Breasted, *Ancient Records of Egypt*, III., 386, n. a.

essential attributes and worship of the nature-goddess throughout Western Asia.[5]

The "origins" of this worship and its ultimate development are not directly relevant to our present enquiry; but we must make passing allusion to a point of special interest and wide significance. As regards Asia Minor, at least, a theory that explains certain abnormal tendencies in worship and in legend would attribute to the goddess, in the primitive conception of her, the power of self-reproduction, complete in herself, a hypothesis justified by the analogy of beliefs current among certain states of primitive society.[6] However that may be, a male companion is none the less generally associated with her in mythology, even from the earliest historical vision of Ishtar in Babylonia,[7] where he was known as Tammuz. While evidence is wanting to define clearly the original position of this deity in relation to the goddess,[8] the general tendency of myth and legend in the lands of Syria and Asia Minor, with which we are specially concerned, reveals him as her offspring,[9] the fruits of the earth. The basis of the myth was

---

5. *Cf. Inter alia*, De Vogüé, *Mélanges d'archéologie orientale*, pp. 45, 46, and Hauvette-Besnault, "Fouilles de Délos," *Bull. Corr. Hell.* (1882), p. 484. *ff.*

6. *Cf.* Frazer, *Adonis, Attis, and Osiris*, pp. 80, 220; Farnell, *Cults of the Greek States*, ii., p. 628, iii., p. 305; Ed. Meyer, *Die Androgyne Astarte, Z. D. M. G.* (1875), p. 730.

7. *Cf.* Pinches, on the Cult of Ishtar and Tammuz, *Proc. S. B. A.*, xxxi. 1909, p. 21.

8. *Cf.* the words, "My son, the fair one" (Pinches, *Proc. S. B. A.* 1895, p. 65, col. 1, l. 9, of the Lamentation). On the other hand, in *W. Asia Inscr.*, ii. pl. 59, 1, 9, Tammuz is said to have been the son of Sirdu. In the epic of Gilgamesh (Ed. Unguad, *Das Gilgamesch-Epos*, 1911, l. 46, 47) Tammuz is described as the Beloved of [Ishtar's] Youth (*cf.* King, *Babylonian Relig.*, p. r60). Cheyne, *Encyc. Bib.*, col. 4,893, pointed out that one interpretation of this name refers to Tammuz as a son of life—true divine child.

9. By some ancient writers Attis was definitely regarded as the son of Kybele, *e.g.*, Schol. on Lucian, *Jupiter Tragædus*, 8 (p. 60, Ed. Rabe); Hippolytus, *Refutatio omn. Haeresium*, v. 9, cited by Frazer, *op. cit.*, p. 219, *q.v.*: *cf.* also Farnell, *Greece and Babylon*, p. 254, and *Cults*, ii., p. 644, iii. 300, etc. The legends appear in Ovid (*Fast.* iv. 295 *ff.*), Pausanias (vii. 17, ix. 10). Though commonly regarded as of shepherd origin (*cf.* Diod. iii., iv., Theocr. xx. 40; Tertul. *de Nat.* i.), he was deified and worshipped in common with Kybele in the Phrygian temples (Paus. vii. xx. 2). It is, of course, to his character or fundamental attributes that we allude in our narrative.

Introduction 3

human experience of nature, particularly the death of plant life with the approach of winter and its revival with the spring. In one version accordingly "Adonis" descends for the six winter months to the underworld, until brought back to life through the divine influence of the goddess. The idea that the youth was the favoured lover of the goddess belongs to a different strain of thought, if indeed it was current in these lands at all in early times. In Asia Minor at any rate the sanctity of the goddess's traditional powers was safeguarded in popular legend by the emasculation of "Attis," and in worship by the actual emasculation of her priesthood,[10] perhaps the most striking feature of her cult. The abnormal and impassioned tendencies of her developed worship would be derived, according to this theory, from the efforts of her worshippers to assist her to bring forth notwithstanding her singleness. However that may be, the mourning for the death of the youthful god, and rejoicing at his return, were invariable features of this worship of nature. It is reasonable to believe that long before the curtain of history was raised over Asia Minor the worship of this goddess and her son had become deep-rooted.

There then appeared the Hittites. In relation with Babylonia and Egypt, these peoples had already become known at the close of the third millennium B.C.;[11] and, to judge from the Biblical accounts, numbers of them had settled here and there throughout Syria and Palestine as early as the days of the patriarchs.[12] Nothing is known of their constitution and organization in these days, however; it is not until their own archives speak that we find them in the fourteenth century B.C. an already established constitutional power, with their capital at Boghaz-Keui.[13] Their sway extended southward into Syria as far as the Lebanon,

---

10. This is not, however, the explanation suggested by Frazer (*op. cit.*, p. 224-237); or by Farnell (*Cults*, iii., pp. 300-301; *Greece and Babylon*, p. 257, and n. 1). On the custom itself, see the stirring poem by Catullus, "The Atys," No. LXIII.

11. King, Chronicles i., pp. 168, 169; Garstang, *Land of the Hittites* (hereafter cited as *L. H.*), p. 323, notes 2, 3; *L. H.* p. 77, p. 1, p. 323, n. 4.

12. Genesis xxiii., xxv. 9, xxvi. 34, xlix. 29, 32. *Cf.* Ezekiel, xvi. 3, 45; *L. H.*, p. 324, n. 2.

13. Winckler, *Mitt. d. Deut. Orient. Ges.*, 1907, No. 35, pp. I, 75. The texts are translated in chronological order by Williams, *Liv. Ann. Arch.*, iv. 1911, pp. 90, 98.

eastward to the Euphrates, and at times into Mesopotamia, westward as far as Lydia, and probably to the sea coast.[14]

Their chief deity was a God omnipotent, the "Lord of Heaven,"[15] with lightning in his hand, the controller of storms ruling in the skies, and, hence identified with the sun. At Senjerli,

Fig. 1.—The Hittite "Hadad" at Malâtia

in the north of Syria, he was represented simply with trident and hammer,[16] the emblems of the lightning and the thunder. But a sculpture at Malâtia, on their eastern frontier, shows him stand-

---

14. *L. H.*, p. 326. The sculptures of Sipylus and Karabel (*ibid.*, pp. 167-173) are evidence of the extension of the Hittites to near the western coast.

15. Egyptian treaty. *Cf. L. H.*, p. 348. The name of the god in Hittite is not known. Among the Vannic tribes it appears as TESHUB; in Syria, etc., as HADAD; indeed the latter is the general Semitic name, for Lehmann-Haupt has shown that the name of the Assyrian storm-god, as ideographically written, should be read 'Adad rather than Ramman. (*Sitz. Berl. Ak. Wis.*, 1899, p. 119.) On points of resemblance to YAHWEH see the suggestive paper by Hayes Ward, *Am. Jour. Sem. Lang. and Lit.*, xxv., p. 175.

16. *L. H.*, pl. lxxvii., p. 291. *Ausgr. in Sendschirli*, pl. xli. (i). On the hammer or axe as an emblem of the thunder, etc., *cf.* Montelius, "The Sun-god's Axe and Thor's Hammer," in *Folk-lore*, xxi., 1910, p. 60.

ing on the back of a bull, the emblem of creative powers,[17] and bearing upon his shoulder a bow, identifying him with a God of Arms, as was natural amongst warlike tribes, His enshrined image is found carved upon a rocky peak of the Kizil Dagh,[18] a

FIG. 2.—THE CHIEF HITTITE GOD AND GODDESS AT BOGHAZ-KEUI

ridge that rises from the southern plains on the central plateau of Asia Minor. In the sanctuary near Boghaz-Keui, clad like their other deities in the Hittite warrior garb, he has assumed a conventional and majestic appearance, bearded, with the lightning emblem in one hand and his sceptre in the other,[19] a prototype of Zeus. The scene of which this sculpture is a part represents the

---

17. Our Fig. 1, *L. H.*, pl. xliv., *Liv. Annals Arch.*, ii. (1909), pl. xli (4). *Cf.* the familiar representation in glyptic art of Hadad leading a bull, *e.g.*, Ward, *Seal Cyl. of West Asia*, Ch. xxx., figs. 456, 459, 461, etc.

18. *Proc. S. B. A.*, 1909 (March), pl. vii.; *L. H.*, p. 180, n. 2. The god is identified by an ideogram in the inscription.

19. See our Fig. 2, drawn from casts exhibited in the Liverpool Public Museums. *Cf. L. H.*, pl. lxv.

ceremonial marriage of the god with the Great Mother,[20] with the rites and festivities that accompanied the celebration, so far as mural decoration permits of treatment of such a theme. From these sculptures we learn that which is fundamental in the Hittite religion, namely, the recognition of a chief god and goddess, and though doubtless the outcome of the political conditions, the mating of these two deities at the proper season would seem to have been peculiarly natural and appropriate to the old established religion of the land. In this union, moreover, each god preserved its dignity and individuality, each cult maintained its proper ceremonies, yet the pair could be worshipped in common as the divine Father and Mother, the source of all life, human, animal, and vegetable.

With the goddess there is in these sculptures the image of the youth[21] who, in the original tradition, was her necessary companion, representing clearly, in this instance, her offspring,

---

20. *L. H.*, p. 239. That this is a divine marriage scene is generally accepted (Frazer, *op. cit.*, p. 108; Farnell, *Greece and Babylon*, p. 264; *cf.* Perrot and Chipiez, *Histoire de l'Art*, iv., p. 630), but it is the recognition that the chief god concerned is not a Tammuz or Attis (as supposed by Frazer, *op. cit.* p. 105; Ramsay, *Journ. Roy. A. S.*, 1885, pp. 113-120, and others), but the Hittite "Zeus," a form of Teshub or Hadad, that is new in our interpretation and important for our present subject. On the general question of the *Hieros Gamos*, *cf.* Daremberg, Saglio and Pottier, *Dictionnaire des Antiquités*, 1904, p. 177; Farnell, *Cults*, i., p. 184 *ff.*; Pausanias, ix., 3; and Frazer, *The Golden Bough* (1890), pp. 102-103. An oriental version of the rite is suggested in the legend recorded by Ælian (*Nat. Animalium*, xii. 30) that Hera bathed in the Chaboras, a tributary of the Euphrates, after her marriage with Zeus. *Cf.* the marriage of Nin-gir-su and Baü in Babylonian mythology (Thu. Dangin, *Vorderas Bibl.*, i., p. 77; *cf.* Jastrow, *Relig. of Bab. and Assyr.*, 1898, p. 59). The details of the scene seem to indicate that the shrine is essentially that of the goddess (*cf.* Kybele as a goddess of caves, Farnell, *Cults*, iii., p. 299, and Ramsay, *Relig. of Anatolia*, in Hastings' *Dict. Bibl.*, extra vol., p. 120), and that the image of the god was carried thereto for this ceremony. (*Cf.* our note 48, p. 77, also Farnell, *Greece and Babylon*, p. 268). It is of interest to recall Miss Harrison's arguments, *Classical Rev.* (1893), p. 24, that Hera had a husband previous to Zeus; also the association of Dodonian Zeus (Homer, *Il.*, xvi. 233; *Od.*, xiv. 327, xvi. 403; Hesiod ap. Strabo, p. 328) with the Earth-Mother in Greece (*cf.* Farnell, *Cults*, i., p. 39).

21. *L. H.*, pl. lxv. Representations of the youthful god are rare (*cf.* Farnell, *Greece and Babylon*, p. 252); the alternative interpretation would be to see in this image an Attis-priest, clad like the god; similarly the second of the two female forms on the double eagle would be the priestess of the goddess in front. This would seem to be made possible by the analogy of a sculpture from Carchemish

Introduction 7

the fruits of the earth.²² Indeed a later sculpture at Ivrîz seems to show this god, changed in form but still recognizable,²³ as the patron of agriculture, with bunches of grapes in one hand and ears of corn in the other. Even at Boghaz-Keui, this youthful deity is already accorded a smaller adjacent sanctuary,²⁴ devoted to his cult alone. Following the great deities are many other figures, forming, as it were, two groups. Accompanying the god are the minor gods of the Hittite States, who, for the most part, are similar to himself in general appearance.²⁵ They are followed by priests and men who are taking part in the celebration, in which it would appear revelry and dancing were not omitted. In the train of the goddess, who like her son stands upon the back of a

FIG. 3.—THE HITTITE BULL-GOD AT EYUK.

(Hogarth, *Liv. Annals. Arch.*, pl. xxxv., i.); but the symbols defining all the figures indicate equally their divine rank. This view is accepted by Frazer, *op. cit.*, p. 106.

22. For the tradition of a son to Atargatis, completing the analogy of a divine triad, see below, n. 70.

23. *L. H.*, pl. lvii. and p. 195. Frazer, *op. cit.*, pp. 98, 100.

24. *L. H.*, pl. lxxi. and p. 241.

25. The first two may be varied aspects of the great god; the seventh is, however, identical with the local deity of Malâtia. *L. H.* pl. xliv. (ii.).

lioness, there follow two other goddesses of smaller size, but similar to herself in appearance, grouped together on a double-headed eagle.[26] These are followed by a number of figures of priestesses clad like the goddess; and, surveying all, the noble figure of the King-Priest clad in a toga-like garment, and holding a curving lituus, the emblem of his sacred office.[27]

That which seems to us in our present enquiry the chief feature of these sculptures is that the worship is clearly common to the god and the goddess, who occupy the leading positions in equal prominence.[28] This interpretation is supported substantially by sculptures which decorate the main entrance of the neighbouring Hittite city of Eyuk. The corner stone on the right represents the goddess seated,[29] receiving the worship of her priests; while the corresponding corner stone on the left shows a Bull-God on a pedestal,[30] with the High Priest and Priestess ministering at his

---

26. *L. H.*, lxv. The double eagle is found at Eyuk: we may see in this group the nature-goddess in a local dual aspect.

27. *L. H.*, pl. lxviii. On his head a cap (*cf.* Lucian, § 42). His kingly rank is denoted by the winged disc surmounting his emblems.

28. That the male god was really dominant would appear from the fact that his name takes first place in the list of Hittite deities in the Egyptian treaty. *L. H.*, p. 348. This agrees with Macrobius' allusion to Hadad of Hierapolis (see below, p. 25). The general prevalence of his worship among the Hittite and kindred peoples is seen in the Hittite archives, the Tell el Amarna tablets, and the Vannic inscriptions. The dual character of the cult is suggested by the seals of the treaty in question, by some of the T. A. letters (*e.g.*, Winckler, Nos. 16, 20, from which the name of the chief goddess among the Mitanni would seem to be accepted as Ishtar), and possibly by the Hittite-Mitanni treaty.

29. *L. H.*, pl. lxxiii.

30. See our Fig. 3. The bull freely replaces the god on coins of Hierapolis, Tarsus, etc. (*B. M. Cat.*, Galatia, etc. *Cf.* also Babélon, *Les Penses Achéménides*, pl. li., vol. 8, pl. xxiv., pp. 20, 22). So also in glyptic art (*cf.* Hayes Ward, *Seal Cyl. of West Asia*, ch. lii.). Both at Eyuk and at Malâtia, in the sculpture described above, rams and goats are seen led to the altar as for sacrifice, and the goat accompanies the leading god at Boghaz-Keui. It is interesting to recall the term αἰγοφάγος applied to Zeus (Farnell, *Cults*, pp. 96, 750, n. 48), and the βουφόνια, a chief rite in the Athenian Diipoleia in the festival of Zeus Polieus. So also in the Cult of Zeus of Attica, a god of agriculture, eating the ox was regarded as a sacrament, the ox p. 11 being regarded as of kin to the worshippers of the god. On Dionysus as a bull and a goat, see Frazer, *The Golden Bough*, V. (1912), ch. ix. *Cf.* also our n. 60, p. 16.

altar. The Bull we have seen to be identified with the chief Hittite deity, which he seems here to replace.

This conclusion is of importance in our present subject, for Lucian (in § 31) describes the chief sanctuary of the great Syrian temple at Hierapolis as containing the common shrine of "Zeus" and "Hera." His very use of these names suggests the wedded character of the deities. Had the shrine been that of the Great Mother alone, the god would not have been accorded an equal prominence near the common altar; he would have been an "Attis," not a "Zeus." The goddess herself would have been in the Greek mind a Rhea or Aphrodite, not a Hera; and Lucian was sufficiently familiar with his subject to be able to discriminate. As it is, he is perplexed in his identification of the goddess by her very comprehensive attributes, which included the many virtues and powers to which the Greek mind assigned separate personifications, known by different names. Speaking generally," he says, "she is undoubtedly Hera, but she has something of the attributes of Athene and of Aphrodite, and of Selene and of Rhea and of Artemis and of Nemesis and of the Fates."

To sum up this stage of our argument, the chief Hittite deity is a god of the skies, identified with the sun; he is all powerful, and in symbolism is identified with the Bull. In formal sculpture he resembles Zeus. The chief Hittite goddess is of comprehensive character: the emblems in her hand and her youthful companion reveal the nature-goddess; while the mural crown, the lion, and double axe are special symbols of the Great Mother surviving with the Phrygian Kybele (or Rhea).[31] The central Hittite cult is that of this mated pair, the Bull-god Zeus and the Lion nature-goddess. The central cult-images of Hierapolis, as described by Lucian, are exactly similar. There are the mated pair of deities: the god is indistinguishable from Zeus,[32] and he is seated on bulls; while the goddess, who is called for brevity "Hera," as the consort

---

31. See note 69 below.
32. *Cf.* § 31, p. 71. "The effigy of Zeus recalls Zeus in all its details—his head, his robes, his throne, nor even if you wished it could you take him for another deity." The term ZEUS-HADAD would aptly describe the Hittite deity: it is suggested by the fact that the god of Hierapolis identified with "Zeus" by Lucian is called "Hadad" by Macrobius. *Cf.* below, p. 19.

of "Zeus," embodies attributes of the nature-goddess or Great Mother, and she is seated on lions.

The central cult at Hierapolis is thus apparently identical with that which the Hittites had established in the land 1500 years before Lucian wrote. It remains to examine such independent evidences as are available from literary and archaeological sources, to see whether they bear out the argument. We shall find our main conclusion remarkably substantiated. But before passing from the evidence of the Hittite monuments, inasmuch as Lucian's narrative is chiefly descriptive of the developed cult of the nature-goddess (with the god submerged), it is of special interest to notice how widespread are the evidences of her worship in the Hittite period. We have spoken of two of her shrines in the interior, at Boghaz-Keui and Eyuk. There is a third at Fraktin, in the mountainous country south of Cæsarea. Here the sculptures are carved on the living rock overlooking a stream.[33] The goddess is represented seated behind an altar on which appears her bird. She seems in this case uniquely to wear the Hittite hat, but the carving is not carried out in detail. Before the altar her priestess is pouring an oblation. The counterpart to this group is a Hittite god and worshipper, while between them is a draped altar of special character.[34] One of the earliest of her images, according to Pausanias,[35] is that which may still be seen on Mount Sipylus, near to Smyrna on the western coast a gigantic figure of the goddess seated, carved in the living rock, and distinguished as Hittite handiwork by certain hieroglyphs carved in the niche.[36] Further east, in Phrygia, one of different character has been found at Yarre.[37] In this sculpture, which is on a movable stone, we have one of a series of representations in which the goddess, seated as always, is worshipped in a ceremonial feast or communion. The funerary character of this class of monument is attested by a similar sculpture from Karaburshlu,[38] near Senjerli, in the north

---

33. *L. H.*, pp. 150, 151 and pl. xlvii.
34. See Fig. 4, and below, p. 18.
35. Paus. iii., xxii. 4.
36. *L. H.*, pp. 168-170 and pl. liii.
37. *Jour. Hell. Stud.*, xix., pp. 40-45 and Fig. 4; *L. H.*, pp. 164-165.
38. *Corp. Inscr. Hit.* (Messerschmidt) (1900), p. 20 and p. xxvi. *L. H.*, pp. 99100, *Cf. ibid.*, p. 100, n. 2.

of Syria, and other illustrations are found at Marash, where the cup, mirror, and girdle are instructive details of the scene.[39] The conception of the Great Mother as goddess of the dead is by no means strained or unnatural, for the resurrection and future life is a dominant theme in the universal myth associated with her. And just as the dead year revived in springtime through her mediation, so she may have been entreated on behalf of the dead for their well-being or their return to life.[40] Thus a second class of similar monument represents the goddess enshrined, with a votary in the act of worship or adoration. Such are the two sculptures at Eyuk, one from Sakje-Geuzi, and three from Marash, in the north of Syria. In one of these, from the last-named place, the goddess is distinguished by the child upon her knee, and a mirror and bird accompany the group, which is further remarkable for the lyre before her upon the altar. In others from this place, a bow appears, held in one case in the hand of the worshipper, who proffers it towards her above the altar as though dedicating it to her service and entreating her blessing. A further sculpture in which the goddess plays a part has been found at Carchemish, but details of the scene are not yet available. Other sculptures, resembling these in general appearance, at Senjerli,[41] Malâtia, and possibly at Boghaz-Keui itself, in which the personages taking part in this ceremonial feast are male and female, may possibly be modifications representing the local king and queen as High Priest and Priestess, or impersonating the god and goddess in the communion rite.

In Glyptic art[42] two varieties of goddess are apparent; the one is robed and seated, and for the most part resembles the deity in her distinctively Hittite character;[43] the other is naked, and she has been supposed to have had her origin in this aspect in

---

39. Humann and Puchstein, *Reisen*, Atlas, pl. xlvii-xlix.; *L. H.*, pp. III-112, 119.
40. The power of Ishtar to raise the dead is implied in her threat to do so, should the door of Hades not be opened to her. *Cf.* Pinches, *Proc. S. B. A.*, xxxi. (1909), p. 26. On Kybele (Matar Kubile) as Goddess of the Dead in Phrygian art, see Ramsay, *Jour. Hell. Stud.*, v., p. 245.
41. *L. H.*, pl. lxxv., No. 1, etc.
42. *Cf.* Hayes-Ward, *The Seal Cylinders of Western Asia*, esply. Chs. xlix., 1.
43. *E.g.*, *ibid.*, No. 898, where she wears the Hittite hat, and the feet of her throne suggest lion's paws. The lion appears definitely below the throne in No.

Syria, whence she penetrated further east.[44] This latter form of goddess has its counterpart in numerous small clay and bronze images, of votive character, which may be found in many places of Northern Syria.[45] In these the goddess is represented as naked, with her hands proffering her breasts. A similar deity, though winged, is represented on a sculptured but undated monument from Carchemish.[46] This is not, however, the Hittite goddess as she is known in Asia Minor, where she is uniformly represented as seated and robed, and commonly wearing a veil which is thrown back from the face. Nor is she the Dea Syria described by Lucian,[47] though commonly identified with her by modern writers. The reason for this identification is probably to be found in the general tendency towards the development of human passions in connection with the Syrian cults, and emphasized in the special characteristics of Astarte of Phœnicia as the goddess presiding over human birth.[48]

The Hittites came and went; their dominion over Asia Minor was subject to repeated onslaughts on every side, from the Egyptians, the Assyrians, the Vannic tribes, the Cimmerians, the Muski and the Phrygians. Their empire, moreover, was held together only insecurely by a system of confederation and alliance which was not apparently of mutual seeking, but imposed by the

---

908. In No. 907, curiously, she stands on a bull. She is accompanied by a bird in these, as in Nos. 904, 908, 943.

44. *Ibid.*, p. 162. The myth of Ishtar's Descent to Hades, however, reveals the goddess naked at one stage of her yearly journey. Ed. Meyer is of opinion (Roscher's *Lexikon*—ASTARTE) that some of the Babylonian clay figures of the naked goddess are archaic and local.

45. Specimens are exhibited in the Hittite gallery of the Liverpool Public Museums.

46. Hogarth, *Liv. Ann. Arch.*, ii. (1909), p. 170, Fig. 1.

47. Atargatis of Hierapolis is always represented as robed on coins of the site, see below, p. 16, and Figs. 5 and 7, also the frontispiece. There is a small bronze figure in the Ashmolean Museum at Oxford (Aleppo, 1889, No. 794), which possibly represents the goddess. The head-dress is debased; but the other features—hair, necklace, dress, and facial expression—are' characteristic and instructive. On the character and relations of the goddess in general, *cf.* Cumont, "Dea Syria," *Real Encyc.* (Wissowa), iv., col. 2237.

48. Prof. Lehmann-Haupt reminds me that the name Mylitta or Mullitta applied to the goddess by Herodotus (I., 131, 199) is derived from *mu'allidatu*: The Giver (or Helper) of Birth.

Hatti during the period of their supremacy at Boghaz-Keui; and from the 12th century B.C. it began rapidly to disintegrate. There is little record of the subsequent events: the Assyrian annals reveal only a series of sporadic coalitions in Syria, to resist their oncoming, and a temporary revival of the Hittite States in that region during the 10th and 9th centuries B.C. Before 700 B.C. the fall of Carchemish, followed by the submission of the region of Taurus and Marash, brought all semblance of Hittite power to an end. What had happened meanwhile in Asia Minor in the struggles between the Phrygians and the Hittites can only be imagined, but in any case by the year 550 B.C., when Crœsus of Lydia crossed the Halys and took possession of Pteria (Boghaz-Keui), he found it still in the hands of a Syro-Cappadocian population: thereafter the political history of Asia Minor becomes largely that of Persia and Macedonia, of Greece and Rome.

With the Hittites fell their chief god from his predominant place in the religion of the interior. Whether, indeed, he did not survive elsewhere than at Hierapolis, in various local guises or legends, noticeably at Doliche,[49] is a problem into which it would

---

49. Doliche is near Aintab, not far north-west from Hierapolis. The worship of Jupiter Dolichenus was introduced to the Roman army by Syrian soldiers (*cf.* Cumont, *Oriental Religions in Roman Paganism*, pp. 113, 117, 147 and 263, n. 23; also in Wissowa's *Real Encyc.* iv., DEA SYRIA, col. 2243). The god stands on a bull holding the lightning and the double axe. (See the illustration in Roscher's *Lexikon*, DOLICHENUS, and especially the fine sculpture at Wiesbaden, published in the *Bonner Jahrbücher*, 1901, pl. viii., and compare with the Hittite Hadad of Malâtia, our Fig. 1). His consort is a lion goddess. She is described on inscriptions (*C. I. L.*, vi. 367, 413) by the name "Hera Sancta," which is parallel to the references to the Syrian goddess on inscriptions found at Delos, where the cult had been established by colonists during the second century B.C. ("Fouilles à Delos," *Bull. Corr. Hell.*, 1882, p. 487); thus (in No. 15), Ἀγνῇ Ἀφροδίτῃ Ἀταργάτι καὶ Ἀδάδου; (No. 18) Ἀταργάτει ἁγνῇ θεῷ; (No. 19) ἁγνῇι θεῶι Ἀταργάτει. (*Cf.* Cumont, DEA SYRIA, *loc. cit.* col. 2240; also the "Zeus Hagios" of a Phœnician coin, p. 18 Hill. *Jour. Hell. Stud.*, xxxi., p. 62). The Anatolian character of the god is recognised by Kan, *De Jovis Dolicheni cultu* (1901), p. 3 *ff. Cf.* also, F. C. Andreas (in Sarre's *D. Oriental. Feldzeichen*), in KLIO III. (1903), pp. 342-343. So, too, the god and goddess of Heliopolis (Baalbek), identified with the bull and lion respectively, resemble the Hadad and Atargatis of Hierapolis and the original Hittite pair of divinities (*cf.* Dussaud in *Rev. Arch.*, 1904, pt. ii., p. 246, etc.). *Cf.* also, the "Jupiter" of the Venasii, Strabo, xii., ii. 6. The subject of the Phœnician and Cilician analogous mated divinities is more complex, but both regions were at one time or another within

be irrelevant to enter. But the Great Mother lived on, being the goddess of the land. Her cult, modified, in some cases profoundly, by time and changed political circumstances, was found surviving at the dawn of Greek history in several places in the interior. Prominent among these sites is Pessinus in Phrygia, a sacred city, with which the legend of Kybele and Attis is chiefly associated. Other districts developed remarkable and even abnormal tendencies in myth and worship. At Comana, in the Taurus, where the Assyrian armies were resisted to the last, and the ancient martial spirit still survives, she became, like Isthar, a goddess of war, identified by the Romans with Bellona:[50] In Syria, again, a different temper and climate emphasized the sensuous tendency of human passions. In all these cases, however, there survived some uniformity of ceremonial and custom. At each shrine numerous priests, called Galli, numbering at Comana as many as 5,000, took part in the worship. Women dedicated their persons as an honourable custom, which in some cases was not even optional, to the service of the goddess. The great festivals were celebrated at regular seasons with revelry, music, and dancing, as they had been of old, coupled with customs which tended to become, in the course of time, more and more orgiastic. These are, however, matters of common knowledge and may be studied in the classical writings. Lucian himself adds considerably to our understanding of these institutions; indeed his tract has been long one of the standard sources of information, supplying details which have been applied, perhaps too freely, to the character of the general cult. Religion in the East is a real part of life, not tending so much as in the West to become stereotyped or conventionalized, but changing with changes of conditions, adapted to the circumstances and needs

---

the Hittite political sphere of influence. An instructive cubical seal from near Tarsus, now in the Ashm. Mus., Oxford (publ. Sayce, *Jour. Arch. Inst.*, 5887, pl. xliv., Messerschmidt, *Corpus Inscr. Hit.*, pl. xliii., i.), shows upon its chief face the two Hittite divinities in characteristic aspect, but the other faces are devoted to the cult of the goddess.

50. An emblem of the priesthood of Bellona was the double axe. *Cf.* Guigniant, *Nouv. Gall. Mythol.*, p. 120; also Montelius, in *Folk Lore*, xxi. (1910), i. p. 60 *ff.*

of the community.[51] So, wherever the goddess was worshipped there would be variety of detail. It is, however, remarkable in this case, that throughout the Hittite period, though wedded and in a sense subordinate to a dominant male deity, and subsequently down to the age at which Lucian wrote, she maintained, none the less, her individuality and comprehensive character. Thus, while Lucian is concerned in his treatise with the cult of an apparently local goddess of northern Syria, we recognize her as a localised aspect of the Mother-goddess, whose worship in remoter times had already been spread wide, and so explain at once the points of clear resemblance in character and in worship to other nature-goddesses of Syria and Asia Minor.

From this general enquiry among the most ancient monuments of the country into the historical origins of the dual cult at Hierapolis, and the character of the goddess, we pass in conclusion to the particular local evidences, more nearly of Lucian's age, that serve to illustrate and amplify his descriptions. There are two chief sources: firstly, the local coins,[52] ranging in date from the time of Alexander down to the 3rd century A.D.; and secondly, the literary allusions of Macrobius, who lived and wrote about A.D. 400. The feature of these branches of evidence that first strikes the enquirer is their obvious reference to a cult and worship which did not change in its essential features throughout the seven centuries of political turmoil which they cover. This enables us to realize how the cult might have been originally established during the remoter days of Hittite supremacy in the land.

The coins are not numerous, but they are profoundly instructive: in particular, one of these, which we shall presently

---

51. *Cf.* the pertinent remarks by Robertson-Smith, *Relig. Sem.*, especially p. 58, on the change of the Mother Goddess from an unmarried to a married state.

52. Our chief sources in this regard have been the coins in the Num. Dept. of the Brit. Mus. and in the Bib. Nationale, Paris; Wroth, *Cat. of Coins of Galatia, Cappadocia, and Syria* (1899); Waddington, in *Revue Numismatique*, (1861). Six, in *Num. Chron.* (1878). Babélon, *Les Perses Achéménides* (1890); Luynes, *Satrapies et Phénicie*, (1846); Neumann, (*Pop. et Regum*) *Numi Veteres inediti* (1783). Hill, on some "Græco-Phoen. Shrines" (*Jour. Hell. Stud.*, xxxi. 9, 11), and "Some Palestinian Cults" (*Proc. Brit. Acad.*, v, 1912). To Mr. Hill we are specially indebted for suggestions and help in this enquiry.

describe, furnishes a direct illustration of Lucian's description of the sanctuary; while two others, which are among the earliest, corroborate in certain details the main point of our argument. In general also, these coins, even those of the later dates, uniformly reveal the goddess as a lion deity; for wherever her full form is shown, she is seated on a lion[53] or on a lion-borne throne.[54] Commonly, however, only her head or bust is given, *e.g.*, in one case, the full face[55] with dishevelled or possibly "radiate" hair; in another, the profile,[56] showing upon her head a mural crown with her veil thrown back. Her name, Atargatis, is recognizable on these coins, though it takes several forms.[57] On this point, therefore, the local evidence confirms the records of Strabo, Pliny, and Macrobius.[58] The male deity has almost disappeared in the later coins, surviving chiefly in his symbol, the bull, which in some cases occurs singly as a counterpart to the lion or lion-goddess on the opposite side of the coin,[59] and in other cases is shown in the grip of the lion as though reminiscent of the ultimate triumph of the cult of the goddess over that of the god.[60] In similar fashion,

---

53. See our frontispiece, No. 8; *Num. Chron., loc. cit.*; also B. M. bronzes, No. 51 (date, *Caracalla*; *cf.* Wroth, *Cat.*, pl. xvii., No. 16).

54. See frontispiece, No. 4, also Fig. 7; *Num. Vet., loc. cit.*; also B. M. bronzes, Nos. 47, 48, 49 (date, *Caracalla*, 198-217 A.D.).

55. *Num. Chron., loc. cit.*, pl. vi., No. 3.

56. 21:56 Our frontispiece, No. 5 (*ibid.*, No. 4).

57. The familiar reading is התערתע (see frontispiece, No. 2, and Fig. 5, p. 20), which is separable without difficulty into עתרת ('Atar), the Aramaic form of תרתשש ('Astarte) and התע ('Até or 'Atheh); reading thus 'Atar-'ate. See note 25, p. 46; and *cf.* Dussaud, "Notes mythol. Syriees," in *Rev. Arch.* (1904), p. 226. The legend התענוכי, Yekun-'ate (Six, *loc. cit.*, No. 3), indicates the separability of 'Ate (Atheh) as a distinct name. The legend on our No. 8, עטהתע, is possibly a contraction of התתע and (הבט. *Cf.* Six, *op. cit.*, p. 107; *cf.* also Movers, *Phœn.*, i., pp. 307, 600. But see Ed. Meyer, *Gesch. des Alth.*, i., pp. 307-308.

58. See p. 19.

59. *E.g.*, Brit. Mus. silver coin of Ant. Pius (Wroth, *Cat., Gal., Cap. and Syria*, pl. xvii., No. 2, also No. 8).

60. *E.g.*, Babélon, *op. cit.*, pl. li., No. 18; *Num. Chron.* (1861), p. 103, rev. Coins of other sites, *e.g.*, Aradus, Byblos, Tarsus, etc., freely illustrate the same themes. *Cf.* the epithet applied to the Lions of Kybele by Sophocles, *Philoktetes*, i. 401 (ἰὼ μάκαιρα ταυροκτόνων λεόντων ἔφεδρε). On this point, see Crowfoot, *J. H. S.*, 1900, p. 118, who argues the theme to be symbolical of the death of the god, whether Attis or Dionysus. So Ishtar, in the epic of Gilgamesh, is

the coins of the Roman Empire show an imperial eagle triumphing above the lion[61] in several examples.

In two cases, however, the figure of the god does survive. One of these coins of the period of Alexander,[62] shows upon the obverse the figure of the god seated upon a throne, holding in his left hand a long sceptre, and in the right hand something which is not distinct. On the reverse side of the coin, the goddess is represented clad in long robes, with girdle, seated upon a lion; she holds in her left hand, it would seem, the lightning trident.[63]

Instructive as this coin is, it yields in interest to another of the 3rd century A.D., in which the two deities are shown seated on their thrones,[64] on either side of a central object, surmounted by a bird, exactly like the picture of the sanctuary, which Lucian describes in § 32. The reverse of the coin bears the legend ΘΕΩΙ CΥPIAC (IEPOΠ)OΛITΩN. The object in the centre is an ædicula, surmounted by a dove, and enclosing apparently a Roman standard.[65] To the right is the god, bearded, clad in a long tunic, with a tall *calathos* on his head, a sceptre in his right hand; he is seated, as it were, upon bulls, but actually upon a throne to which the head and forepart of bulls form the side-piece. On the right-hand side, Atargatis, the Syrian Goddess, is seated similarly upon a throne which two lions support; she is clothed and girdled, and wears a broad *calathos* or crown upon her head. In the field of the coin, below these representations, there appears a lion. The subject of this coin, is, as we have said, an actual illustration of Lucian's description of the sanctuary: his words are as follows:—"In this shrine are placed the statues, one of which is Hera, the other Zeus, though they call him by another name.

---

accused of being the cause of the death of Tammuz, and of her lion (Ungnad, *Das Gilgamesch Epos*, p. 31, ll. 52 f).

61. *Cf.* Wroth, *op. cit.*, pl. xvii., etc.

62. Frontispiece, No. 8; published by Six, *Num. Chr.* (1878), pl. vi., p. 104, No. 2.

63. We have discussed the legend of this coin in n. 57. M. Six (*loc. cit.*), following Movers, accepts the theoretical reading "Baal-Kevan" as the name of the god.

64. See our Fig. 7, p. 70. Publ. *Numi vet.*, pt. ii., tab. iii., 2.

65. Six (*Num. Chron.*, *loc. cit.*, p. 119) describes the object as a legionary eagle; but this is somewhat misleading.

Both are sitting; Hera is supported by lions, Zeus is sitting on bulls. . . . Between the two there stands another image of gold, no part of it resembling the others: this possesses no special form of its own, but recalls the characteristics of the other gods. The Syrians speak of it as Semeïon [σημήϊον],[66] its summit is crowned by a golden pigeon." It is only in reference to this central object that the description fails, though, in both cases, a bird is perched upon the top; and doubtless therefore, the design upon the coin is intended to illustrate something similar to that which Lucian describes. The object upon the coin is formal, architectural, and

FIG. 4.—HITTITE DRAPED ALTAR-PEDESTAL: FRAKTIN

Roman in character; while Lucian tells us particularly that the object between the deities "recalled characteristics of the other gods." We are reminded by this reference of a feature in Hittite sculptures, notably those at Fraktin. Here the pillars of the altars of the goddess and of the god take the form of a human body from the waist downwards, swathed in many folds of a fringed

---

66. Professor Bosanquet suggests that the Greek word was possibly used in the sense of the Latin *Signum*.

garment or robe; and upon the altar of the goddess appears a bird, doubtless a pigeon or dove, which was in all tradition her peculiar emblem.[67] Lucian's description is more aptly explained by this symbolism: the object as seen upon the coin had clearly become conventionalized in Roman times. However that may be, the dual character of the cult, the god identified with the bull, the goddess with the lion, is remarkably substantiated.

Further instructive details with regard to these deities are given by Macrobius, and we may appropriately quote from him the following significant passage[68]:—"The Syrians give the name *Adad* to the god, which they revere as first and greatest of all; his name signifies 'The One.' They honour this god as all powerful, but they associate with him the goddess named *Adargatis*, and assign to these two divinities supreme power over everything, recognizing in them *the sun* and *the earth*. Without expressing by numerous names the different aspects of their power, their predominance is implied by the different attributes assigned to the two divinities. For the statue of *Adad* is encircled by descending rays, which indicate that the force of heaven resides in the rays which the sun sends down to earth: the rays of the statue of *Adargatis* rise upwards, a sign that the power of the ascending rays brings to life everything which the earth produces. Below this statue are the figures of lions, emblematic of the earth; for the same reason that the Phrygians so represent the Mother of the gods, that is to say, the earth, borne by lions." The character, then, of the god and goddess in the sanctuary of the temple, the heart of the cult, remained still the same in the fourth century A.D. as it had been in the beginning. The words which Macrobius uses would be equally descriptive of the special attributes of the Hittite Sun-God and the Hittite Earth-Goddess, which we have described, and the reference to Cybele of Phrygia is also significant.[69] There is indeed a faint memory in tradition of a

---

67. See pp. 11, 12, and n. 65, p. 88.
68. "Saturnalia": end of Ch. xxiii.
69. In general aspect the Phrygian goddess is indeed hardly distinguishable from the Hierapolitan goddess as described by Lucian. Compare our illustration of Rhea or Kybele, from a Roman lamp (Fig. 8, p. 73), with the representation in Fig. 7, p. 72. This resemblance is further seen in a relief in the Vatican (*Vatican*

son to Atargatis,[70] corresponding to the youthful companion of the Hittite goddess at Boghaz-Keui, and hence doubtless to the "Tammuz" and "Attis" of the various legends; and in one of the effigies at Hierapolis it is possible to see a later aspect of this deity corresponding to the Hittite Sandan-Hercules of Ivrîz.[71]

If any doubt remained as to the historical origins of the cult at Hierapolis, it would be dispelled by another coin, one of the earliest of the site, on the face of which is the picture and name of the goddess, Atargatis.[72] On the reverse of the coin is seen

Atargatis, the Syrian Goddess.

Abd-Hadad, the Priest-King.

FIG. 5.—COIN OF HIERAPOLIS, DATE B. C. 332. (NOW IN THE BIBL. NATIONALE, PARIS.)

Kat., i., Plates, Gall.-Lapidara, Tf. 30, No. 152), described in C. I. L., vi., No. 423: "Superne figura Rheæ cornu copiæ, timone, modio ornatæ, stans inter duos leones"—which, however, Drexler (in Roscher's Lexikon, I., col. 1991) proposes to identify with Atargatis rather than Rhea.

70. Xanthos the Lydian relates that "Atargatis" was taken prisoner by the Lydian Mopsus and thrown into the lake at Ascalon (sacred to Derceto; see n. 25, p. 52), with her son Ἰχθύς (Athen. viii. 37). On the proposed identification of the son with Simios, the lover of Atargatis (Diod. ii. 4), etc., see Dussaud, Rev. Arch. (1904), ii., p. 257, who indicates the analogy of the "Hierapolitan triad, Hadad, Atargatis and Simios," with the Heliopolitan, Jupiter, Venus and Mercury. He believes (p. 259) the triad of Hadad to have been of Babylonian origins, implanted at Hierapolis, to reign there through Syria, Palestine and Phœnicia. "Il ne nous appartient pas de rechercher ses migrations et ses influences en Asie Mineure." There is an interesting representation of a Syrian triad in the Ashmolean Museum, Oxford (1912, 83).

71. See n. 47, p. 75.

72. See our Fig. 5, and frontispiece, No. 2. Publ. Num. Chron., p. 105, No. 5. Choix de Mon. Grecq, pl. xi. 24; Rev. Arch. (1904), ii., pl. 240, Fig. 24 (photo).

the priest-dynast of the age (about 332 B.C.): his name is Abd-Hadad, the "servant of Hadad." He is represented at full length, but owing to the wearing of the coin, some of the details are lost. The robe upon him, however, recalls that of the Hittite priest; and the hat which he wears is unmistakably the time-honoured conical hat distinctive of the Hittite peoples. Except in such local religious survival as is here illustrated, this hat must have long fallen into disuse.

In short, the words of Macrobius, which corroborate and amplify Lucian's description of the central cult at Hierapolis, are strictly apposite to the chief Hittite god and goddess. The coins of the site illustrate the same motive; and on one of the earliest of them, features of Hittite costume are found still surviving four hundred years after the final overthrow of the Hittite States in Northern Syria.

J. G.

LIFE OF LUCIAN

There is no ancient biography of Lucian extant excepting an unsatisfactory sketch by Suidas; but we can gather many facts as to his life from his own writings. He expressly tells us that he was a Syrian or Assyrian, and that Samosata was his native place, the capital of Commagene, situated on the right or western bank of the Euphrates. He was probably born about the year 125 A.D., and his career extends over the greater part of the second century after the Christian era. He was of humble extraction; he tells us that his mother's family were hereditary sculptors (λιθοξόοι). This fact is interesting as enabling us to suppose that he would examine with an accurate and critical eye the different statues which he saw and described in his various travels, and especially those in the great temple at Hierapolis. He tells us, however, that he proved but a sorry sculptor, and nothing was left him but to apply himself to the study of literature and to adopt the profession of a sophist. He could not even, according to his own account, speak pure Greek, and with the view of purifying his language he visited successively the rhetorical schools of Ionia and Greece proper, where he made the acquaintance of the Platonic philosopher Nigrinus, and no doubt contracted much of the admiration for Plato which reveals itself in his writings. We see him next at Antioch practising as a lawyer in the Courts; he enjoyed in this capacity such a reputation for oratory that he felt entitled to gratify his spirit of restlessness and intellectual curiosity by travel, and adopting the career of a travelling sophist. In this capacity he visited Syria, Phœnicia and Egypt, probably in the years 148 and 149 A.D. He tells us in the *De Dea Syria* that he had been at Hierapolis, Byblus, Libanus, and Sidon; and we know from his own description how carefully he inspected these great seats of Oriental beliefs.

He likewise tells us that he visited Egypt, but that he went to no other part of Libya. He arrived at Rome about 150 A.D., suffering from bad eyesight and anxious to consult a good oculist. After a sojourn of two years in Italy he passed into Gaul, where he had heard that there was a good opening for a public lecturer, and here he stayed for some ten years. He learned so much while among the Gauls that he was able to retire from the profession of lecturer and to devote himself to the study of philosophy. He returned to the East through Macedonia, staying to lecture at Thessalonica, and travelling through Asia Minor reached Samosata in 164 A.D. There he found his father still living, and removed him and his family to Greece, whither he followed them in the following year. On his way he visited Abonoteichos, afterwards Ionopolis, in Cappadocia, where he visited the false prophet Alexander, and nearly met his end owing to a trick played upon him by that impostor. He passed by Aegialos and proceeded to Amastris, whence he travelled into Greece with Peregrinus Proteus, and he says that he was present when that most marvellous of charlatans burnt himself alive at Olympia. He then settled down at Athens, devoting himself to the study of philosophy, and he seems to have passed a happy and prosperous life of learned leisure. At the end of the century he found his resources failing and once more betook himself to the employment of his youth; and he was glad to be relieved from this drudgery by a good and lucrative appointment conferred on him by the Emperor Severus in connexion with the Law Courts of Alexandria. Of the date of his death we know nothing.

The tract on "The Syrian Goddess" is thought to have been one of his earliest works, written when he was fresh from the East, as appears among other things from his calling Deucalion by his Syrian name, Σκύθης, meaning Σικύδης, *i.e.*, Xisuthrus.[1] It has been doubted by some scholars whether this tract was really by Lucian, on the ground that it is written in the Ionic dialect, the employment of which Lucian derides in *Quomodo Historiam*, § 18. But the scholiast on the Nubes of Aristophanes certainly

---

1. See the references in Müller and Donaldson, Vol. III., p. 223, from whose work most of these facts have been taken.

ascribes it to Lucian, and it is quite in keeping with the versatility of his genius to adopt a style at an early period of his literary career, and, at a later period to mock at the affectations of his early productions. In any case, whether the tract is by Lucian or not, it gives a singular picture of the beliefs and practices in Hierapolis, and is worthy of the attention of archæologists and students of comparative religions.

"Lucian was at one time secretary to the prefect of Egypt, and he boasts that he had a large share in writing the laws and ordering the justice of that province. Here this laughing philosopher found a broad mark for his humour in the religion of the Egyptians, their worship of animals and water-jars, their love of magic, the general mourning through the land on the death of the bull Apis, their funeral ceremonies, their placing their mummies round the dinner table as so many guests, and pawning a father or a brother when in want of money."—Sharpe's *History of Egypt*, Chap. xv., § 51.

It is especially noteworthy that he wrote this treatise in the Ionic dialect in imitation of Herodotus, who adopted that form of Greek for his great work, and it speaks much for the powers of Lucian as a linguist and as a stylist that he was able to pass from the Ionic dialect to the pure Attic Greek in which the rest of his works are composed.

It is no part of our aim to criticise Lucian fully as an author; it will be plain from the short sketch of his life that he was singularly attracted by the spirit of curiosity to obtain all possible information about the strange Oriental cults among which he had been brought up. He gives us information at first hand on the religion of the Assyrians, and much of this is of extreme interest as tallying with what we read in the Old Testament. The flood which destroyed all mankind for their wickedness; the salvation of one man and his family; the animals which went into the ark in pairs; the special sanctity ascribed to pigeons among the Syrians, all recall memories of Jewish traditions. Stratonice's guilty love for Combabus and his rejection of her advances recall other passages of the Old Testament; and the consecration of their first beard and their locks by the young men and maidens respectively recalls passages in Catullus and Vergil, and seems to show that

this custom was an importation from the East. The tract on the Dea Syria differs from Lucian's other works by its simplicity and freedom from persiflage. It is the work of an intelligent traveller conversant with architecture and with the technique of statuary, and anxious to record the facts that he had been able to ascertain as to the strange Oriental cults practised in his native country. His attitude is that of an interested sceptic, but he confesses himself unable to explain all the miracles which he witnessed at Hierapolis, though he probably deemed that they owed their existence to some tricks of the priests such as he had seen performed on other occasions.

The following passage from one of a series of lectures to clergy at Cambridge[2] may be added to this brief account:—

"It is the peculiar distinction of Lucian in the history of letters that he was the first to employ the form of dialogue, not on grave themes, but as a vehicle of comedy and satire. He intimates this claim in the piece entitled *The Twice Accused*, which is so called because Lucian is there arraigned by personified Rhetoric on the one part and by Dialogue on the other. Rhetoric upbraids him with having forsaken her for the bearded Dialogus, the henchman of philosophy: while Dialogus complained that the Syrian has dragged him from his philosophical heaven to earth, and given him a comic instead of a tragic mask. Lucian's dialogues blend an irony in which Plato had been his master with an Aristophanic mirth and fancy. His satire ranges over the whole life of his time, and he has been an originating source in literature. His true history is the prototype of such works as *Gulliver's Travels*: his *Dialogues of the Dead* were the precursors of Landor's Imaginary Conversations."

Müller and Donaldson quote Sir Walter Scott as affirming that "from the *True History of Lucian* Cyrano de Bergerac took his idea of a Journey to the Moon, and Rabelais derived his yet more famous *Voyage of Pantagruel*."

As the tract *De Dea Syria* is mainly descriptive it is unnecessary here to enter fully into Lucian's views of religion and philosophy. It may, however, be remarked that the belief in reli-

---

2. *Essays and Addresses* (Cambridge University Press, 1907).

gion, whether as represented by the ancient and national gods of Rome and Greece, or by the Oriental deities, had lost its hold on both the educated and uneducated classes. The disappearance of religion was succeeded by superstition in various forms, which was exploited to their own advantage by such charlatans and adventurers as Alexander and Peregrinus Proteus. Lucian's attitude is that of a detached and scornful observer, who, however, in spite of his contempt for the silliness of his fellow men, sees the pathos of human affairs, and would fain make them regard conduct as the standard of life. Professor Dill[3] has remarked that the worldly age in which Lucian's lot was cast was ennobled by a powerful protest against worldliness. This protest was none other than the lives of the best of the philosophers who waged unceasing war against selfishness and superstition in a selfish and superstitious age. Lucian mocks indeed at these philosophers without, however, apparently having thought it worth his while to study any system of philosophy very deeply. "Yet the man who was utterly sceptical as to the value of all philosophic effort, in the last resort approaches very nearly to the view of human life which was preached by the men whom he derides. . . . There are many indications in the dialogues that if Lucian had turned Cynic preacher he would have waged the same war on the pleasures and illusory ambitions of man, he would have outdone the Cynics in brutal frankness of exposure and denunciation, as he would have surpassed them in rhetorical and imaginative charm of style."

Lucian has heard of Christianity, but seems to have regarded it as an ordinary Oriental cult. He refers to it twice; the first passage is in the memoirs of Alexander, in which the false prophet is alleged to have proclaimed: "If any atheist, Christian, or Epicurean has come to spy out the sacred rites, let him flee"; and in the same tract (§ 25) he couples Christians and atheists. The second passage is in the treatise on the death of Peregrinus the impostor, who, according to Lucian, was a renegade from Christianity and indeed had occupied an important post among that community. The translation is Sir Richard Jebb's.

---

3. See *Roman Society from Nero to Marcus Aurelius* (Macmillan, 1905), p. 339.

"He had thoroughly learnt," says Lucian, "the wondrous philosophy of the Christians, having consorted in Palestine with their priests and scribes. What would you expect? He speedily showed that they were mere children in his hands: he was their prophet, the chief of their religious fraternity (θιασιάρχης), the convener of their meetings (συναγωγεύς) —in short, everything to them. Some of their books he interpreted and elucidated; many of them he wrote himself. They regarded him as a god, made him their law-giver, and adopted him as their champion (προστάτην ἐπεγράφοντο)."

Concerning their tenets he says, "They still reverence that great one (τὸν μέγαν ἐκεῖνον), the man who was crucified in Palestine because he brought this new mystery into the world. The poor creatures have persuaded themselves that they will be altogether immortal and live for ever; wherefore they despise death and in many cases give themselves to it voluntarily. Then their first Law-giver (*i.e.*, Christ) persuaded them that they were all brethren, when they should have taken the step of renouncing all the Hellenic gods, and worshipping that crucified one, their sophist, and living after his laws. So they despise all things alike (*i.e.*, all dangers and sufferings) and hold their goods in common: though they have received such traditions without any certain warrant. If then an artful impostor comes among them, an adroit man of the world, he very soon enriches himself by making these simple folk his dupes."

It is fair to say that by some writers of repute[4] Peregrinus is regarded as a conscientious mystic, and Lucian as unqualified to understand mysticism and religious enthusiasm. In any case it is clear that Lucian for all the scorn with which he regards the various religions and philosophies of his age, showed considerable interest in collecting facts about them, and those which he gives us in the tract on *The Syrian Goddess* are as instructive as any.

The tract on *The Syrian Goddess* has been translated at the instance of the Liverpool Institute of Archæology. The text followed is that of Dindorf (Paris, 1884). The memoir on Lucian

---

4. *E.g.*, Mr. T. R. Glover in *The Conflict of Religions in the Early Roman Empire*, p. 212.

is mainly based upon the *History of the Literature of Ancient Greece* (Müller and Donaldson), Sir Richard Jebb's "Lucian" in his *Essays and Addresses* (Cambridge University Press), Sir Samuel Dill's *Roman Society from Nero to Marcus Aurelius*, and Glover's *Conflict of Religions in the Early Roman Empire*.

H. A. S.

Fig. 6.—Temple at Byblos
B. M. Cat. Coins, Phœn. Byb. 32.
Date A.D. 217-8.

LUCIAN'S "DE DEA SYRIA"

ANALYSIS OF THE SUBJECT-MATTER

§		PAGE
	INTRODUCTORY	
1.	The Sacred City	35
2.	Origins of Temples and Shrines	35
	THE OLDEST SHRINES AND CULTS OF SYRIA	
3.	Hercules of Tyre	37
4.	The Phœnician Astarte at Sidon. Legend of Europa	37
6.	Aphrodite of Byblos and the Legend of Adonis	39
7.	Legend of Osiris at Byblos	41
8.	The Adonis River; its red colour	41
9.	Cult of Aphrodite in the Lebanon at Aphaca	43
10.	Hierapolis: The greatest Sanctuary. Its Pilgrims	43
	LEGENDS OF FOUNDATION	
12.	Ascribed by some to Deukalion. Story of the Deluge	45
13.	Story of the Chasm	45
14.	Assigned by others to Semiramis. Derceto, the Fish-Goddess	47
15.	By others again to the Lydian Attis	49
16.	Lucian shares the View that it was founded by Dionysus	51
17.	Re-built by Stratonice	53
19.	Story of Stratonice and Combabus	55

§	DESCRIPTION OF THE TEMPLE AND SHRINES	
31.	The Inner Sanctuary. The Effigies	71
32.	Comprehensive Character of the Goddess	71
33.	Object between the God and Goddess	73
34.	The Sun God	75
35.	A Bearded Apollo	75
36.	Image of the God borne by the Priests in Divination	77
38.	Atlas and other Images	79
41.	Sacred Animals	81
42.	The Priests and Temple Attendants	81
	RITES AND CEREMONIES	
44.	The Sacrifices	81
45.	Sacred Lake and Fishes	83
47.	Ceremony at the Lake	83
48.	Ceremony at the Euphrates ("The Sea")	85
49.	Festival of the Pyre	85
	CUSTOMS AND INSTITUTIONS	
50.	The Galli	87
51.	Their Initiation Ceremonies	87
52.	Their Burial	87
54.	Animals used in Sacrifice. Sanctity of the Dove	89
55.	Tonsure and other Customs of Pilgrims	89
57.	Method of Sacrifice. The Libation	91
58.	Human Sacrifice	91
59.	Tattoo	91
60.	Sacrifice of Hair	91

ΠΕΡΙ ΤΗΣ ΣΥΡΙΗΣ ΘΕΟΥ

1. Ἔστιν ἐν Συρίῃ πόλις οὐ πολλὸν ἀπὸ τοῦ Εὐφρήτεω ποταμοῦ, καλέεται δὲ Ἰρή, καὶ ἔστιν ἱρὴ τῆς Ἥρης τῆς Ἀσσυρίης. δοκέει δέ μοι, τόδε τὸ οὔνομα οὐκ ἅμα τῇ πόλει οἰκεομένῃ ἐγένετο, ἀλλὰ τὸ μὲν ἀρχαῖον ἄλλο ἦν, μετὰ δὲ σφίσι τῶν ἱρῶν μεγάλων γιγνομένων ἐς τόδε ἡ ἐπωνυμίη ἀπίκετο. περὶ ταύτης ὦν τῆς πόλιος ἔρχομαι ἐρέων ὁκόσα ἐν αὐτῇ ἐστιν· ἐρέω δὲ καὶ νόμους τοῖσιν ἐς τὰ ἱρὰ χρέωνται, καὶ πανηγύριας τὰς ἄγουσιν καὶ θυσίας τὰς ἐπιτελέουσιν. ἐρέω δὲ καὶ ὁκόσα καὶ περὶ τῶν τὸ ἱρὸν εἰσαμένων μυθολογέουσι, καὶ τὸν νηὸν ὅκως ἐγένετο. γράφω δὲ Ἀσσύριος ἐών, καὶ τῶν ἀπηγέομαι τὰ μὲν αὐτοψίῃ μαθών, τὰ δὲ παρὰ τῶν ἱρέων ἐδάην, ὁκόσα ἐόντα ἐμεῦ πρεσβύτερα ἐγὼ ἱστορέω.

2. Πρῶτοι μὲν ὦν ἀνθρώπων τῶν ἡμεῖς ἴδμεν Αἰγύπτιοι λέγονται θεῶν τε ἐννοίην λαβεῖν καὶ ἱρὰ εἵσασθαι καὶ τεμένεα καὶ πανηγύριας ἀποδεῖξαι. πρῶτοι δὲ καὶ οὐνόματα ἱρὰ

---

1. Identified with the ruins of modern Mumbidj, on a route from Aleppo to the junction of the Sajur River with the Euphrates, from which point it is distant 14½ miles (23 kilometres). *Cf.* Smith's *Dict. of Greek and Roman Geog.*—HIERAPOLIS. The distance accords with that given by a fifth century pilgrim, ? Etheria [Silvia]; *cf. Corp. Script. Eccl. Lat.*, xxxix. p. 61, cited by Hogarth, *Jour. Hell. Stud.*, xiv. (1907-8), p. 183. Strabo (xvi. i. 28) gives the distance as four *schœni* from the river. For early explorers' descriptions of the site, see quotations in the Appendix, pp. 95-99. Many of the fine remains of Roman, Saracenic, Seljukian and Moslem times are now in ruins, but the sacred lake and other features are still to be seen (see note 55).

2. *Cf.* § 31. By the words "Assyrian Hera" Lucian tersely identifies the goddess and distinguishes her attributes:—"Hera," because mated (§ 31) to a "Zeus ", "Assyrian," because she is to be distinguished from the classical conception of the deity. For this use of the term Assyrian in the sense of North Syrian (or Aramaean), *cf.* Rob.-Smith, *Eng. Hist. Rev.*, 1887, pp. 312, 313; and note Lucian's reference to himself below as an "Assyrian born." On the name of the goddess, Atargatis, which appears on local coins and is mentioned by Strabo, Pliny, Macrobius, etc., see Introduction, pp. 1, 16; and note 25 below.

3. Its name in Hittite and subsequent Assyrian period has not been recognised. "Bambyce" seems to be the earliest name substantiated, and it came

On the Syrian Goddess

1. There is in Syria a city not far from the river Euphrates:[1] it is called "the Sacred City," and is sacred to the Assyrian Hera.[2] As far as I can judge this name was not conferred upon the city when it was first settled, but originally it bore another name.[3] In course of time the great sacrifices were held therein, and then this title was bestowed upon it. I will speak of this city, and of what it contains. I will speak also of the laws which govern its holy rites, of its popular assemblies and of the sacrifices offered by its citizens. I will speak also of all the traditions attaching to the founders of this holy place: and of the manner of the founding of its temple. I write as an Assyrian born[4] who have witnessed with mine own eyes some of the facts which I am about to narrate: some, again, I learnt from the priests: they occurred before my time, but I narrate them as they were told to me.

2. The first men on earth to receive knowledge of the gods, and to build temples and shrines and to summon meetings for religious observances are said to have been the Egyptians.[5] They were the first, too, to take cognizance of holy names, and to repeat

---

to be called "Hierapolis" ("the sacred city") by the Greeks. Strabo (xvi. i. 28) mentions another name, Edessa, but this is an obvious error. Pliny states that the local Syrian name was Mabog, *Nat. Hist.* v. 23 (19), § 81 (Ed. Detlefsen).

4. "An Assyrian born"—actually born about A.D. 125 at Samsat, on the Euphrates. The place in Hittite times, of which there are traces [*cf.* Land of the Hittites (hereafter cited *L. H.*), pp. 130, 131; *Corp. Inscr. Hit.* (1900), p. 14, pl. xvii.; Humann and Puchstein, *Reisen*, Atlas, pl. xlix. 1-3], was on the Mitannian and later the Assyrian frontier, and by the Assyrians several times attacked, as in 1120 B.C. and again about 885 B.C. About 750 B.C. it was in possession of the Vannic kings, and it was finally annexed to the Assyrian empire about 743 B.C. Nineveh fell to the Medes in 606. After the period of Persian domination it became first capital of the province of Commagene in the Greek kingdom of Syria. The district was later ruled by independent princes of Seleucid extraction. Subsequently the seat of government was transferred to Hierapolis.

5. Archæological research hardly bears out this statement. *Cf. inter alia* Hilprecht, *Exploration in Bible Lands* (1903); King and Hall, *Egypt and Western Asia in the Light of Recent Discoveries* (1907). *Cf.* Herodotus, ii. 2 *et seq.*

ἔγνωσαν καὶ λόγους ἱροὺς ἔλεξαν. μετὰ δὲ οὐ πολλοστῷ χρόνῳ παρ' Αἰγυπτίων λόγον Ἀσσύριοι ἐς θεοὺς ἤκουσαν, καὶ ἱρὰ καὶ νηοὺς ἤγειραν, ἐν τοῖς καὶ ἀγάλματα ἔθεντο καὶ ξόανα ἐστήσαντο.

3. τὸ δὲ παλαιὸν καὶ παρ' Αἰγυπτίοισιν ἀξόανοι νηοὶ ἔσαν. καὶ ἔστιν ἱρὰ καὶ ἐν Συρίῃ οὐ παρὰ πολὺ τοῖς Αἰγυπτίοισιν ἰσοχρονέοντα, τῶν ἐγὼ πλεῖστα ὄπωπα, τό γε τοῦ Ἡρακλέος τὸ ἐν Τύρῳ, οὐ τούτου τοῦ Ἡρακλέος τὸν Ἕλληνες ἀείδουσιν, ἀλλὰ τὸν ἐγὼ λέγω πολλὸν ἀρχαιότερος καὶ Τύριος ἥρως ἐστίν.

4. Ἔνι δὲ καὶ ἄλλο ἱρὸν ἐν φοινίκῃ μέγα, τὸ Σιδόνιοι ἔχουσιν. ὡς μὲν αὐτοὶ λέγουσιν, Ἀστάρτης ἐστίν· Ἀστάρτην δ' ἐγὼ δοκέω Σεληναίην ἔμμεναι. ὡς δέ μοί τις τῶν ἱρέων ἀπηγέετο, Εὐρώπης ἐστὶν τῆς Κάδμου ἀδελφεῆς· ταύτην δὲ ἐοῦσαν Ἀγήνορος τοῦ βασιλέως θυγατέρα, ἐπειδή τε ἀφανὴς ἐγεγόνεεν, οἱ Φοίνικες τῷ νηῷ ἐτιμήσαντο καὶ λόγον ἱρὸν ἐπ' αὐτῇ ἔλεξαν, ὅτι ἐοῦσαν καλὴν Ζεὺς ἐπόθεεν καὶ τὸ εἶδος ἐς ταῦρον ἀμειψάμενος ἥρπασεν καί μιν ἐς Κρήτην φέρων ἀπίκετο. τάδε μὲν καὶ τῶν ἄλλων Φοινίκων ἤκουον, καὶ τὸ νόμισμα τῷ Σιδόνιοι χρέωνται τὴν Εὐρώπην ἐφεζομένην ἔχει τῷ ταύρῳ τῷ Διί· τὸν δὲ νηὸν οὐκ ὁμολογέουσιν Εὐρώπης ἔμμεναι.

---

6. Hercules of Tyre. *Cf.* Herodotus, ii. 44, who records the local tradition that the temple was 2,300 years old, and convinced himself that this Hercules was a god of very great antiquity. Rawlinson (*Hist. of Phœnicia*, p. 330) points out his identity with Melkarth, who originally represented one aspect of Baal. Similarly the Hittite god represented in the rock sculpture at Ivriz in Asia Minor (*L. H.*, pl. lvii. and pp. 192-195) was identified by the Greeks with Hercules; and is recognised by Frazer (*Adonis, Attis and Osiris*, p. 97) as identical with the Baal of Tarsus. *Cf.* also Ramsay, *Luke the Physician*, pp. 171-179, and a note in his *Pauline and other Studies*, pp. 172-173, and note 47 below.

7. The Phœnician Astarte ['Astart], the goddess of productivity in Nature, particularly in the animal world, and hence the guardian of births. Like the Dea Syria, she is differentiated only by local custom or tradition from other aspects of the Mother-goddess. As the natural consort and counterpart of Baal, who embodied the generative principle, "bringing all things to life everywhere," and thus regarded as the sun-god, she was queen of heaven, and hence the moon-goddess. Another symbolism connected with the legend which follows makes her

sacred traditions. Not long after them the Assyrians heard from the Egyptians their doctrines as to the gods, and they reared temples and shrines: in these they placed statues and images.

3. Originally the temples of the Egyptians possessed no images. And there exist in Syria temples of a date not much later than those of Egypt, many of which I have seen myself, for instance, the temple of Hercules in Tyre.[6] This is not the Hercules of Greek legend; but a Tyrian hero of much greater antiquity than he.

4. There is likewise in Phœnicia a temple of great size owned by the Sidonians. They call it the temple of Astarte.[7] I hold this Astarte to be no other than the moon-goddess. But according to the story of one of the priests this temple is sacred to Europa, the sister of Cadmus. She was the daughter of Agenor, and on her disappearance from Earth the Phœnicians honoured her with a temple and told a sacred legend about her; how that Zeus was enamoured of her for her beauty, and changing his form into that of a bull carried her off into Crete.[8] This legend I heard from other Phœnicians as well; and the coinage current among the Sidonians bears upon it the effigy of Europa sitting upon a bull, none other than Zeus.[9] Thus they do not agree that the temple in question is sacred to Europa.

---

the Cow-goddess in relation to the Bull-god. *Cf.* Robertson-Smith, *Religion of the Semites*, p. 477. These purely feminine attributions reflect a patriarchal state of society, with the male god dominant. (*Cf.* the interesting remarks by Rob. Smith in the *Eng. Hist. Rev.*, 1887, p. 316.) Among the Greeks and Romans, who recognised in Baal their Zeus or Jupiter, the goddess appeared most like to Aphrodite or Venus, whose prototype she was. She is the Ashtoreth for whom Solomon erected a shrine (2 Kings, ii. 5, 33), which was defiled by Josiah (2 Kings, xxiii. 13), who "brake in pieces the images and cut down the groves." In cult and in name she is the local form of the Babylonian Ishtar, see Introduction, pp. 1, 12.

8. *Cf.* Herodotus, i. 4, iv. 45; Pausanias, vii. 4, i.; ix. 19, i., etc.

9. Zeus, as a bull-god; see also the allusion in § 31, where the "Zeus" of Hierapolis is represented sitting on bulls, as a counterpart to the goddess who is seated on lions. For the identification of the Hittite "Zeus" with the bull, see Introduction, pp. 4, 8; and Figs. 2, 3; *cf.* Fig. 7.

5. Ἔχουσι δὲ καὶ ἄλλο Φοίνικες ἱρόν, οὐκ Ἀσσύριον ἀλλ' Αἰγύπτιον, τὸ ἐξ Ἡλίου πόλιος ἐς τὴν Φοινίκην ἀπίκετο. ἐγὼ μέν μιν οὐκ ὄπωπα, μέγα δὲ καὶ τόδε καὶ ἀρχαῖόν ἐστιν.

6. Εἶδον δὲ καὶ ἐν Βύβλῳ μέγα ἱρὸν Ἀφροδίτης Βυβλίης, ἐν τῷ καὶ τὰ ὄργια ἐς Ἄδωνιν ἐπιτελέουσιν· ἐδάην δὲ καὶ τὰ ὄργια. λέγουσι γὰρ δὴ ὦν τὸ ἔργον τὸ ἐς Ἄδωνιν ὑπὸ τοῦ συὸς ἐν τῇ χώρῃ τῇ σφετέρῃ γενέσθαι, καὶ μνήμην τοῦ πάθεος τύπτονταί τε ἑκάστου ἔτεος καὶ θρηνέουσι καὶ τὰ ὄργια ἐπιτελέουσι καὶ σφίσι μεγάλα πένθεα ἀνὰ τὴν χώρην ἵσταται. ἐπεὰν δὲ ἀποτύψωνταί τε καὶ ἀποκλαύσωνται, πρῶτα μὲν καταγίζουσι τῷ Ἀδώνιδι ὅκως ἐόντι νέκυι, μετὰ δὲ τῇ ἑτέρῃ ἡμέρῃ ζώειν τέ μιν μυθολογέουσι καὶ ἐς τὸν ἠέρα πέμπουσι καὶ τὰς κεφαλὰς ξύρονται ὅκως Αἰγύπτιοι ἀποθανόντος Ἄπιος. γυναικῶν δὲ ὁκόσαι οὐκ ἐθέλουσι ξύρεσθαι, τοιήνδε ζημίην ἐκτελέουσιν· ἐν μιῇ ἡμέρῃ ἐπὶ πρήσει τῆς ὥρης ἵστανται· ἡ δὲ ἀγορὴ μούνοισι ξείνοισι παρακέαται, καὶ ὁ μισθὸς ἐς τὴν Ἀφροδίτην θυσίη γίγνεται.

---

10. *Cf.* "The city stood on a height a little distance from the sea" (Strabo, xvi. ii. 18). The temple is figured on coins from the site (see our illustration, Fig. 6; and *cf.* Hill on "Some Græco-Phœnician Shrines," in *Jour. Hell. Stud.*, xxxi., 1911, pl. iii., No. 16, etc.). The outer court was approached by steps, and its interior was screened to view from without. It had a façade of columns, and was enclosed by a pilastered wall or cloister. It was open to the sky and a conical obelisk rising from the interior symbolised the cult. The sanctuary was raised by a further flight of steps; its approach was ornamented with pilasters, cornice and pediment, and a roof protected the altar and shrine within (*cf.* Perrot and Chipiez, *Histoire*, iii. 60, Engl. transl. *Phœn.*, p. 61; Rawlinson, *Phœnicia*, p. 146; Evans, *Mykenæan Tree and Pillar Cult*, p. 40; Frazer, *Adonis*, p. 11, note 1, with bibl.). The temples at Hierapolis and at Carchemish were similarly approached by steps.

11. Differing, if at all, only by local attributes from the Sidonian Astarte. *Cf.* Cicero, *De natura deorum*, iii. 23, 59; also see, for a useful summary of the argument, Bennett, *Relig. Cults associated with the Amazons* (New York, 1912), p. 50.

12. For the myth of Adonis, with bibl., see Frazer, *Adonis, Attis, and Osiris*, Ch. i. p. 46 The legend of the wild boar does not survive in the story of Tammuz, but it appears in one version of the death of Attis. It suggests a totemistic origin.

5. The Phœnicians have also another sacred custom, derived from Egypt, not from Assyria: it came, they say, from Heliopolis into Phœnicia. I never witnessed this myself, but it is important, and of great antiquity.

6. I saw too at Byblos a large temple,[10] sacred to the Byblian Aphrodite[11]: this is the scene of the secret rites of Adonis: I mastered these. They assert that the legend about Adonis and the wild boar is true,[12] and that the facts occurred in their country, and in memory of this calamity they beat their breasts and wail every year, and perform their secret ritual amid signs of mourning through the whole countryside. When they have finished their mourning and wailing, they sacrifice in the first place to Adonis, as to one who has departed this life: after this they allege that he is alive again, and exhibit his effigy to the sky. They proceed to shave their heads,[13] too, like the Egyptians on the loss of their Apis. The women who refuse to be shaved have to submit to the following penalty, viz., to stand for the space of an entire day in readiness to expose their persons for hire. The place of hire is open to none but foreigners, and out of the proceeds of the traffic of these women a sacrifice to Aphrodite is paid.[14]

---

13. *Cf.* §§ 55 and 60 below. On the custom of hair-offering among the Semites, *cf.* Robertson-Smith, *Relig. Semites*, p. 325 *ff.*; also Frazer, *Adonis*, etc., p. 34.

14. A custom of similar character commonly attached itself to the worship of the Great Mother in her various forms (*cf.* Herod. i. 199; Strabo, xv. i. 20), being regarded as an honourable devotion to her service (Strabo, xi. xiv. 16); it was obligatory in Lydia (Herodotus, i. 93). *Cf., inter alia*, Ramsay, *Cities and Bishoprics of Phrygia*, i. 94, 115; Cumont, in *Pauly's Real-Encyclopädie* (Wissowa), 1901, iv., DEA SYRIA, col. 2242; Frazer, *Fortnightly Review*, Dec., 1904, p. 985. For the survival of the custom on old Hittite sites, *cf.* Strabo, xii. iii. 32, 34, 36; *ibid.* ii. 3, etc.). Belin de Ballu, *Œuvres de Lucien*, v. p. 141, n. 1, cites a similar custom obligatory before marriage (Chez les Angiles, peuples d'Afrique, dont parla Pomponius Méla, liv. I, ch. 8). *Cf.* also the comprehensive review of the question by Farnell, *Greece and Babylon*, p. 269 *ff*, and the valuable *résumé* by Cumont in his *Religions Orientales*, p. 319, n. 41. The significance of the connection with a stranger as a relic of exogamy is discussed by Perrot and Chipiez, *Histoire de l'Art*, *Phénicie*, pp. 258-261, and developed by S. Reinach, *Myth. Cultes*, I. (1905), p. 79. But *cf.* Frazer, *Adonis*, etc., p. 50 *ff.*

7. Εἰσὶ δὲ ἔνιοι Βυβλίων οἳ λέγουσι παρὰ σφίσι τεθάφθαι τὸν Ὄσιριν τὸν Αἰγύπτιον, καὶ τὰ πένθεα καὶ τὰ ὄργια οὐκ ἐς τὸν Ἄδωνιν ἀλλ᾽ ἐς τὸν Ὄσιριν πάντα πρήσσεσθαι. ἐρέω δὲ καὶ ὁκόθεν καὶ τάδε πιστὰ δοκέουσι. κεφαλὴ ἑκάστου ἔτεος ἐξ Αἰγύπτου ἐς τὴν Βύβλον ἀπικνέεται πλώουσα τὸν μεταξὺ πλόον ἑπτὰ ἡμερέων, καί μιν οἱ ἄνεμοι φέρουσι θείῃ ναυτιλίῃ· τρέπεται δὲ οὐδαμά, ἀλλ᾽ ἐς μούνην τὴν Βύβλον ἀπικνέεται. καὶ ἔστι τὸ σύμπαν θωῦμα. καὶ τοῦτο ἑκάστου ἔτεος γίγνεται, τὸ καὶ ἐμεῦ παρεόντος ἐν Βύβλῳ ἐγένετο· καὶ τὴν κεφαλὴν ἐθεησάμην Βυβλίνην.

8. Ἔνι δὲ καὶ ἄλλο θωῦμα ἐν τῇ χώρῃ τῇ Βυβλίῃ. ποταμὸς ἐκ τοῦ Λιβάνου τοῦ οὔρεος ἐς τὴν ἅλα ἐκδιδοῖ· οὔνομα τῷ ποταμῷ Ἄδωνις ἐπικέαται. ὁ δὲ ποταμὸς ἑκάστου ἔτεος αἱμάσσεται καὶ τὴν χροιὴν ὀλέσας ἐσπίπτει ἐς τὴν θάλασσαν καὶ φοινίσσει τὸ πολλὸν τοῦ πελάγεος καὶ σημαίνει τοῖς Βυβλίοις τὰ πένθεα. μυθέονται δὲ ὅτι ταύτῃσι τῇσι ἡμέρῃσιν ὁ Ἄδωνις ἀνὰ τὸν Λίβανον τιτρώσκεται, καὶ τὸ αἷμα ἐς τὸ ὕδωρ ἐρχόμενον ἀλλάσσει τὸν ποταμὸν καὶ τῷ ῥόῳ τὴν ἐπωνυμίην διδοῖ. ταῦτα μὲν οἱ πολλοὶ λέγουσιν. ἐμοὶ δέ τις ἀνὴρ Βύβλιος ἀληθέα δοκέων λέγειν ἑτέρην ἀπηγέετο τοῦ πάθεος αἰτίην. ἔλεγεν δὲ ὧδε· «ὁ Ἄδωνις ὁ ποταμός, ὦ ξεῖνε, διὰ τοῦ Λιβάνου ἔρχεται· ὁ δὲ Λίβανος κάρτα ξανθόγεώς ἐστιν. ἄνεμοι ὦν τρηχέες ἐκείνῃσι τῇσι ἡμέρῃσι ἱστάμενοι τὴν γῆν τῷ ποταμῷ ἐπιφέρουσιν ἐοῦσαν ἐς τὰ μάλιστα μιλτώδεα, ἡ δὲ γῆ μιν αἱμώδεα τίθησιν· καὶ τοῦδε τοῦ πάθεος οὐ τὸ αἷμα, τὸ λέγουσιν, ἀλλ᾽ ἡ χώρη αἰτίη.» ὁ μέν μοι Βύβλιος τοσάδε ἀπηγέετο·

---

15. The apparent identity is discussed by Frazer, *Adonis, Attis, and Osiris*, pp. 357, etc. Prof. Newberry tells us that there are instructive points of relationship traceable in the early evidences of the Cult of Osiris in Egypt. The familiar conception of Osiris, however, as King of the Dead, is, in our opinion, traceable to ancestor- and king-worship.

16. *Cf.* Plutarch, *Isis et Osiris*, pp. 12-20 *et seq.* The legend is rendered by Frazer, *op. cit.*, pp. 270-273.

17. The Adonis, or *Nahr Ibrahim*, is a short river flowing down from the Lebanon through precipitous gorges rich in foliage, and entering the sea just

7. Some of the inhabitants of Byblos maintain that the Egyptian Osiris is buried in their town, and that the public mourning and secret rites are performed in memory not of Adonis, but of Osiris.[15] I will tell you why this story seems worthy of credence. A human head comes every year from Egypt to Byblos,[16] floating on its seven days' journey thence: the winds, by some divine instinct, waft it on its way: it never varies from its course but goes straight to Byblos. The whole occurrence is miraculous. It occurs every year, and it came to pass while I was myself in Byblos, and I saw the head in that city.

8. There is, too, another marvellous portent in the region of the Byblians. A river, flowing from Mount Libanus, discharges itself into the sea: this river bears the name of Adonis.[17] Every year regularly it is tinged with blood, and loses its proper colour before it falls into the sea: it dyes the sea, to a large space, red:[18] and thus announces their time of mourning to the Byblians. Their story is that during these days Adonis is wounded, and that the river's nature is changed by the blood which flows into its waters; and that it takes its name from this blood. Such is the legend vulgarly accepted: but a man of Byblos, who seemed to me to be telling the truth, told me another reason for this marvellous change. He spoke as follows: "This river, my friend and guest, passes through the Libanus: now this Libanus abounds in red earth. The violent winds which blow regularly on those days bring down into the river a quantity of earth resembling vermilion. It is this earth that turns the river to red. And thus the change in the river's colour is due, not to blood as they affirm, but to the nature of the soil."[19] This was the story of the Byblian.

---

south of Gebal (Byblos), a short distance only northwards from Beyrout. All visitors are impressed by the grandeur and beauty of its valley, particularly in the higher reaches.

18. *Cf.* Maundrell, *Journey from Aleppo to Jerusalem*, (1699, 6th edit., p. 35), March 17: "The water was stained to a surprising redness, and as we observed in travelling, had discoloured the sea a great way into a reddish hue, occasioned doubtless by a sort of minium, or red earth, washed into the river by the violence of the rain."

19. This is the correct explanation.

εἰ δὲ ἀτρεκέως ταῦτα ἔλεγεν, ἐμοὶ μὲν δοκέει κάρτα θείη καὶ τοῦ ἀνέμου ἡ συντυχίη.

9. Ἀνέβην δὲ καὶ ἐς τὸν Λίβανον ἐκ Βύβλου, ὁδὸν ἡμέρης, πυθόμενος αὐτόθι ἀρχαῖον ἱρὸν Ἀφροδίτης ἔμμεναι, τὸ Κινύρης εἴσατο, καὶ εἶδον τὸ ἱρόν, καὶ ἀρχαῖον ἦν.
10. Τάδε μέν ἐστι τὰ ἐν τῇ Συρίῃ ἀρχαῖα καὶ μεγάλα ἱρά. τοσούτων δὲ ἐόντων ἐμοὶ δοκέει οὐδὲν τῶν ἐν τῇ ἱρῇ πόλει μέζον ἔμμεναι οὐδὲ νηὸς ἄλλος ἁγιώτερος οὐδὲ χώρη ἄλλη ἱροτέρη. ἔνι δὲ ἐν αὐτῷ καὶ ἔργα πολυτελέα καὶ ἀρχαῖα ἀναθήματα καὶ πολλὰ θωύματα καὶ ξόανα θεοπρεπέα. καὶ θεοὶ δὲ κάρτα αὐτοῖσιν ἐμφανέες· ἱδρώει γὰρ δὴ ὧν παρὰ σφίσι τὰ ξόανα καὶ κινέεται καὶ χρησμηγορέει, καὶ βοὴ δὲ πολλάκις ἐγένετο ἐν τῷ νηῷ κλεισθέντος τοῦ ἱροῦ, καὶ πολλοὶ ἤκουσαν. ναὶ μὴν καὶ ὄλβου πέρι ἐν τοῖσιν ἐγὼ οἶδα πρῶτόν ἐστιν· πολλὰ γὰρ αὐτοῖσιν ἀπικνέεται χρήματα ἔκ τε Ἀραβίης καὶ Φοινίκων καὶ Βαβυλωνίων καὶ ἄλλα ἐκ Καππαδοκίης, τὰ δὲ καὶ Κίλικες φέρουσι, τὰ δὲ καὶ Ἀσσύριοι. εἶδον δὲ ἐγὼ καὶ τὰ ἐν τῷ νηῷ λάθρῃ ἀποκέαται, ἐσθῆτα πολλὴν καὶ ἄλλα ὁκόσα ἐς ἄργυρον ἢ ἐς χρυσὸν ἀποκέκριται. ὁρταὶ μὲν γὰρ καὶ πανηγύριες οὐδαμοῖσιν ἄλλοισιν ἀνθρώπων τοσαίδε ἀποδεδέχαται.

11. Ἱστορέοντι δέ μοι ἐτέων πέρι, ὁκόσα τῷ ἱρῷ ἐστιν, καὶ τὴν θεὸν αὐτοὶ ἥντινα δοκέουσιν, πολλοὶ λόγοι ἐλέγοντο, τῶν οἱ μὲν ἱροί, οἱ δὲ ἐμφανέες, οἱ δὲ κάρτα μυθώδεες, καὶ ἄλλοι βάρβαροι, οἱ μὲν τοῖσιν Ἕλλησιν ὁμολογέοντες· τοὺς ἐγὼ πάντας μὲν ἐρέω, δέκομαι δὲ οὐδαμά.

---

20. Probably at Aphaca, now Afka, near the source of the *Nahr Ibrahim*, where the cult was maintained until the time of Constantine, who destroyed the shrine owing to the licentious nature of the orgies in vogue (Eusebius, *Vita Constantina*, iii. 55). At the present day little survives of the ancient buildings except some Roman ruins.

21. This widespread tribute to the shrine of Hierapolis at once reveals the Dea Syria as an aspect of the Great Mother, who under various names was

But even assuming that he spoke the truth, yet there certainly seems to me something supernatural in the regular coincidence of the wind and the colouring of the river.

9. I went up also from Byblos into the Libanus, a single day's journey, as I had heard that there was an ancient temple of Aphrodite there founded by Cinyras. I saw the temple,[20] and it was indeed old.

10. These then are the ancient great temples of Syria. Of all these temples, and they are numerous indeed, none seems to me greater than those found in the sacred city; no shrine seems to me more holy, no region more hallowed. They possess some splendid masterpieces, some venerable offerings, many rare sights, many striking statues, and the gods make their presence felt in no doubtful way. The statues sweat, and move, and utter oracles, and a shout has often been raised when the temple was closed; it has been heard by many. And more: this temple is the principal source of their wealth, as I can vouch. For much money comes to them from Arabia, and from the Phœnicians and the Babylonians: the Cilicians, too, and the Assyrians bring their tribute.[21] And I saw with my own eyes treasures stored away privately in the temple; many garments, and other valuables, which are exchanged for silver or gold. Nowhere among mankind are so many festivals and sacred assemblies instituted as among them.

11. On enquiring the number of years since the temple was founded, and whom they deemed the goddess to be, many tales were told to me, some of which were sacred, and some public property; some, again, were absolutely fabulous; others were mere barbarians' tales; others again tallied with the Greek accounts. All these I am ready to narrate, though I withhold my acceptance of some.

---

worshipped in the several countries mentioned by Lucian, namely, in Arabia as 'Athtar [a male equivalent, *vide* Robertson-Smith, *Relig. Semites*, p. 58], in Phœnicia as 'Astart (Ashtoreth), in Babylonia and Assyria (in varying characters) as Ishtar. Hierapolis, with its hordes of pilgrims, its living worship and frenzied ceremonies, must have been like the Mecca of to-day.

12. Οἱ μὲν ὦν πολλοὶ Δευκαλίωνα τὸν Σκύθεα τὸ ἱρὸν εἵσασθαι λέγουσιν, τοῦτον Δευκαλίωνα ἐπὶ τοῦ τὸ πολλὸν ὕδωρ ἐγένετο. Δευκαλίωνος δὲ πέρι λόγον ἐν Ἕλλησιν ἤκουσα, τὸν Ἕλληνες ἐπ' αὐτῷ λέγουσιν. ὁ δὲ μῦθος ὧδε ἔχει.

Ἥδε ἡ γενεή, οἱ νῦν ἄνθρωποι, οὐ πρῶτοι ἐγένοντο, ἀλλ' ἐκείνη μὲν ἡ γενεὴ πάντες ὤλοντο, οὗτοι δὲ γένεος τοῦ δευτέρου εἰσί, τὸ αὖτις ἐκ Δευκαλίωνος ἐς πληθὺν ἀπίκετο. ἐκείνων δὲ πέρι τῶν ἀνθρώπων τάδε μυθέονται: ὑβρισταὶ κάρτα ἐόντες ἀθέμιστα ἔργα ἔπρησσον, οὔτε γὰρ ὅρκια ἐφύλασσον οὔτε ξείνους ἐδέκοντο οὔτε ἱκετέων ἠνείχοντο, ἀνθ' ὧν σφίσιν ἡ μεγάλη συμφορὴ ἀπίκετο. αὐτίκα ἡ γῆ πολλὸν ὕδωρ ἐκδιδοῖ καὶ ὄμβροι μεγάλοι ἐγένοντο καὶ οἱ ποταμοὶ κατέβησαν μέζονες καὶ ἡ θάλασσα ἐπὶ πολλὸν ἀνέβη, ἐς ὃ πάντα ὕδωρ ἐγένοντο καὶ πάντες ὤλοντο, Δευκαλίων δὲ μοῦνος ἀνθρώπων ἐλίπετο ἐς γενεὴν δευτέρην εὐβουλίης τε καὶ τοῦ εὐσεβέος εἵνεκα. ἡ δέ οἱ σωτηρίη ἥδε ἐγένετο: λάρνακα μεγάλην, τὴν αὐτὸς εἶχεν, ἐς ταύτην ἐσβιβάσας παῖδάς τε καὶ γυναῖκας ἑωυτοῦ ἐσέβη: ἐσβαίνοντι δέ οἱ ἀπίκοντο σύες καὶ ἵπποι καὶ λεόντων γένεα καὶ ὄφιες καὶ ἄλλα ὁκόσα ἐν γῇ νέμονται, πάντα ἐς ζεύγεα. ὁ δὲ πάντα ἐδέκετο, καί μιν οὐκ ἐσίνοντο, ἀλλά σφι μεγάλη διόθεν φιλίη ἐγένετο. καὶ ἐν μιῇ λάρνακι πάντες ἔπλευσαν ἔστε τὸ ὕδωρ ἐπεκράτεεν. τὰ μὲν Δευκαλίωνος πέρι Ἕλληνες ἱστορέουσι.

13. Τὸ δὲ ἀπὸ τούτου λέγεται λόγος ὑπὸ τῶν ἐν τῇ ἱρῇ πόλει μεγάλως ἄξιος θωυμάσαι, ὅτι ἐν τῇ σφετέρῃ χώρῃ χάσμα μέγα ἐγένετο καὶ τὸ σύμπαν ὕδωρ κατεδέξατο: Δευκαλίων δέ, ἐπεὶ τάδε ἐγένετο, βωμούς τε ἔθετο καὶ νηὸν

---

22. This version of the deluge, though associated by Lucian's Greek informants with Deucalion, is clearly of eastern origin, having little resemblance to the Greek legend, and much in common with the Babylonian versions, viz., the story of Xisuthros, recorded by Berosus, and partly preserved; the legend of Tsīt-napishtim in the epic of Gilgamesh, preserved on seventh century tablets from the library of Assurbanipal (and independently appearing on tablets of a king of the first dynasty of Babylon, dating from about 2100 B.C.); and lastly with the Biblical

12. The people, then, allege that it was Deukalion the Scythian who founded the temple; I mean the Deukalion in whose time the great flood occurred. I have heard the story about Deukalion as the Greeks narrate it from the Greeks themselves. The story runs as follows:

The present race of men was not the first to be created. The first generation perished to a man; the present is a second creation. This generation became a vast multitude, owing to Deukalion. Of the men of the original creation they tell this tale: they were rebellious, and wilful, and performed unholy deeds, disregarding the sanctity of oaths and hospitality, and behaving cruelly to suppliants; and it was for these misdeeds that the great destruction fell upon them. Straightway the earth discharged a vast volume of water, and the rivers of heaven came down in streams and the sea mounted high. Thus everything became water, and all men perished; Deukalion alone was saved for another generation, on the score of his wisdom and piety. The manner of his salvation was as follows: He placed his children and his wives in an ark of vast size, and he himself also entered in. Now, when he had embarked, there came to him wild boars and horses, and generations of lions and serpents, and all the other beasts which roam the earth, all in couples. He welcomed them all. Nor did they harm him; and friendship remained amongst them as Zeus himself ordained. These, one and all, floated in this ark as long as the flood remained. This is the legend of Deukalion as told by the Greeks.[22]

13. But a further story is told by the men of Hierapolis, and a wonderful one it is; they say that in their country a mighty chasm appeared which received all the water, and that Deukalion on this occurrence reared altars and founded a temple

---

story of Noah in Genesis. A fundamental difference is that in the Greek legend only Deucalion and Pyrrha were saved, and mankind was subsequently renewed miraculously in response to the oracle of Themis. Lucian's account of the animals coming in couples has its parallel in the Babylonian text: "With all living seed of every kind I filled it, . . . the cattle of the field, and the beasts of the field, . . . all of them I brought in" (transl. by King, *Babylonian Religion*, p. 132. *q.v.*).

ἐπὶ τῷ χάσματι Ἥρης ἅγιον ἐστήσατο. ἐγὼ δὲ καὶ τὸ χάσμα εἶδον, καὶ ἔστιν ὑπὸ τῷ νηῷ κάρτα μικρόν. εἰ μὲν ὦν πάλαι καὶ μέγα ἐὸν νῦν τοιόνδε ἐγένετο, οὐκ οἶδα: τὸ δὲ ἐγὼ εἶδον, μικρόν ἐστιν. Σῆμα δὲ τῆς ἱστορίης τόδε πρήσσουσιν. δὶς ἑκάστου ἔτεος ἐκ θαλάσσης ὕδωρ ἐς τὸν νηὸν ἀπικνέεται. φέρουσι δὲ οὐκ ἱρέες μοῦνον, ἀλλὰ πᾶσα Συρίη καὶ Ἀραβίη, καὶ πέρηθεν τοῦ Εὐφρήτεω πολλοὶ ἄνθρωποι ἐς θάλασσαν ἔρχονται καὶ πάντες ὕδωρ φέρουσιν, τὸ πρῶτα μὲν ἐν τῷ νηῷ ἐκχέουσι, μετὰ δὲ ἐς τὸ χάσμα κατέρχεται, καὶ δέκεται τὸ χάσμα μικρὸν ἐὸν ὕδατος χρῆμα πολλόν. τὰ δὲ ποιέοντες Δευκαλίωνα ἐν τῷ ἱρῷ τόνδε νόμον θέσθαι λέγουσι συμφορῆς τε καὶ εὐεργεσίης μνῆμα ἔμμεναι.

14. Ὁ μὲν ὦν ἀρχαῖος αὐτοῖσι λόγος ἀμφὶ τοῦ ἱροῦ τοιόσδε ἐστίν. ἄλλοι δὲ Σεμίραμιν τὴν Βαβυλωνίην, τῆς δὴ πολλὰ ἔργα ἐν τῇ Ἀσίῃ ἐστίν, ταύτην καὶ τόδε τὸ ἕδος εἵσασθαι νομίζουσιν, οὐκ Ἥρῃ δὲ εἵσασθαι ἀλλὰ μητρὶ ἑωυτῆς, τῆς Δερκετὼ οὔνομα. Δερκετοῦς δὲ εἶδος

---

23. For a further reference to this custom, see § 48. "The Sea" in this regard is to be interpreted as the Euphrates River, as explained by Philostratus, *Vita Apol.*, i. 20; cf. Rob. Smith, *Engl. Hist. Rev.*, 1887, p. 312.

24. Semiramis, mythical founder with Ninus of Nineveh; daughter of the fish goddess Derceto; confused in myth or identified with Ishtar (Astarte). The legends of Semiramis are given by Diodorus (ap. Ctesias), II. i. The historical character of Semiramis and her identity with Sammuṙamat, wife of Samsi-Adad (c. B.C. 820)—son of the Assyrian king Shalmeneser II.—mother of Adad-nirari III., and the development of the myth from historical origins, have been recently demonstrated by Lehmann-Haupt, "Die Hist. Semiramis and ihre Zeit" (*D. O. G.*, Publ. Tübingen, 1910), on the basis of a new inscription of hers found at Assur, together with that from Nimroud, in which her name appears. The student will find early but instructive contributions on the subject by Rob.-Smith and Sayce in the *Engl. Hist. Rev.*, 1887, p. 303, and 1888, p. 504.

25. Derceto, identified with Atargatis by Pliny, *Nat. Hist.* v. 19; indeed, the two names are linguistically similar. That Atargatis was the name of the goddess worshipped at Hierapolis is stated by Strabo (xvi. i. 27), and confirmed by the local coins and other sources (see Introduction, p. 16, and note 57). Atargatis, according to the scholiast on Germanicus' "Aratus," was of local origins, being born in the Euphrates, like Aphrodite from the foam of the sea. (*Cf.* Rob.-Smith, *Relig. Semites*, p. 175, and notes on § 45 below.) The name Atargatis is a compound of ATHAR (Phœn. 'Astart, Heb. 'Ashtoreth) with

to Juno above this chasm. I have actually seen this chasm, it lies beneath the temple and is of very small dimensions. If it was once of large size, and was afterwards reduced to its present small dimensions, I know not: but the chasm which I saw is certainly very small.

They maintain that their tale is proved by the following occurrence; twice in every year the water comes from the sea to the temple. This water is brought by the priests; but besides them, all Syria and Arabia and many from beyond the Euphrates go down to the sea; one and all bring its water which they first pour out in the temple; [23] then this water passes down into the chasm which, small though it be, holds a vast quantity of water. Thus then they act, and they declare that the following law was passed by Deukalion in that temple, in order that it might be an everlasting remembrance at once of the visitation and of its alleviation.

14. Such is their ancient account of the temple. Others again maintain that Semiramis[24] of Babylon, who has left many mighty works in Asia, founded this edifice as well; nor did she dedicate it to Hera, but to her own mother, whose name was Derceto.[25]

'ATTI or 'ATTAH (*vide* Kœnig in Hasting's *Abrig. Dict.*, p. 70 b); or in Aramaic 'ATHAR and 'ATHE (*cf.* Ed. Meyer, *Geschichte des Alterthums*, i., 1st ed., p. 246, § 205 *ff.*). Frazer (*Adonis, etc.*, pp. 529, 130) points out that the compound according to this derivation includes the name of the Cilician goddess 'Ateh, consort of Baal, as well as that of Astarte or Ishtar, amounting thus to Ishtar-Ateh, the latter being presumably a Cilician aspect of the former. Thus far there is no difficulty; but Pliny further describes the goddess as "monstrous" (*prodigiosa*), and his identification with Derceto suggests the familiar fish goddess of Askalon. Moreover, travellers have seen local representations of the characteristic "mermaid" form (see note 26). Yet in what follows Lucian is careful to distinguish Derceto from the "Hera" of Hierapolis, who is seated on a lion-throne (§ 31), and never assumes any fish-like or other monstrous aspect on the local coins. (*Cf.* also Dussaud, in *Rev. Archéologique*, 5904, ii. p. 258.) Assuming the identity of Atargatis with Derceto to be correct, it is more consistent with Lucian's observations (§§ 1, 14-16, 31, 32), and with the argument developed in our Introduction, to see embodied in Atargatis that local aspect of the great Nature-goddess that typified the productive powers of waters (in generating fishes, etc.), and that in this capacity she was accorded at Hierapolis a separate shrine and rites, which none the less formed a part of the general worship of the Universal Mother. It is interesting to speculate how all strains of evidence would be reconciled and explained if it could be shown that "Atheh" was really a local fish-goddess. On the whole question, see further Cumont, "Dea Syria," in Pauly's *Real-Encyclopädie* (Wissowa), 1901, iv., col. 2236, ff.

ἐν Φοινίκῃ ἐθεησάμην, θέημα ξένον· ἡμισέη μὲν γυνή, τὸ δὲ ὁκόσον ἐκ μηρῶν ἐς ἄκρους πόδας ἰχθύος οὐρὴ ἀποτείνεται. ἡ δὲ ἐν τῇ ἱρῇ πόλει πᾶσα γυνή ἐστιν, πίστιες δὲ τοῦ λόγου αὐτοῖσιν οὐ κάρτα ἐμφανέες. ἰχθύας χρῆμα ἱρὸν νομίζουσιν καὶ οὔκοτε ἰχθύων ψαύουσι· καὶ ὄρνιθας τοὺς μὲν ἄλλους σιτέονται, περιστερὴν δὲ μούνην οὐ σιτέονται, ἀλλὰ σφίσιν ἥδε ἱρή. τὰ δὲ γιγνόμενα δοκέει αὐτοῖς ποιέεσθαι Δερκετοῦς καὶ Σεμιράμιος εἵνεκα, τὸ μὲν ὅτι Δερκετὼ μορφὴν ἰχθύος ἔχει, τὸ δὲ ὅτι τὸ Σεμιράμιος τέλος ἐς περιστερὴν ἀπίκετο. ἀλλ᾽ ἐγὼ τὸν μὲν νηὸν ὅτι Σεμιράμιος ἔργον ἐστὶν τάχα κου δέξομαι· Δερκετοῦς δὲ τὸ ἱρὸν ἔμμεναι οὐδαμὰ πείθομαι, ἐπεὶ καὶ παρ᾽ Αἰγυπτίων ἐνίοισιν ἰχθύας οὐ σιτέονται, καὶ τάδε οὐ Δερκετοῖ χαρίζονται.

15. Ἔστιν δὲ καὶ ἄλλος λόγος ἱρός, τὸν ἐγὼ σοφοῦ ἀνδρὸς ἤκουσα, ὅτι ἡ μὲν θεὴ Ῥέη ἐστίν, τὸ δὲ ἱρὸν Ἄττεω ποίημα. Ἄττης δὲ γένος μὲν Λυδὸς ἦν, πρῶτος δὲ τὰ ὄργια τὰ ἐς Ῥέην ἐδιδάξατο. καὶ τὰ Φρύγες καὶ Λυδοὶ καὶ Σαμόθρακες ἐπιτελέουσιν, Ἄττεω πάντα ἔμαθον.

---

26. *Cf.* Maundrell, *Journey from Aleppo to the Euphrates* (1699), relates that he saw "on the side of a large well a stone with three figures carved on it, in *Basso Relievo*. They were two Syrens, which, twining their fishy tails together, made a seat, on which was placed sitting a naked woman, her arms and the Syrens on each side mutually entwined" (Appendix, p. 95). This sculpture was apparently seen also by Pocock, who describes it as a stone about four feet long and three wide, on which there was a relief of two winged persons holding a sheet behind a woman, a little over her head; they seem to carry her on their fishy tails which join together, and were probably designed to represent the Zephyrs, carrying Venus to the sea (quoted in the Appendix, p. 96).

Other famous Syrian shrines of Derceto were at Carnion and Askelon, and at the latter also her effigy represented a mermaid (Hastings, *Abr. Dict.*, p. 70). On the general subject, see Cumont, in *Pauly's Real-Ency.*, "Dea Syria," iv., col. 2237; Robertson-Smith, *Religion of the Semites*, pp. 174-5; also Dussaud, *op. cit.*, p. 243.

27. We take this to refer to the effigy of the Dea Syria (*vide* § 31, etc.). We must not forget, however, the small figure of the naked goddess supported by "mermaids" noticed by Maundrell and Pocock.

28. *Cf.* § 45, and see note 56. The origins of this custom are interestingly discussed by Cumont, Les *Religions Orientales*, p. 357, note 36, where he quotes

On the Syrian Goddess 49

Now, I have seen the semblance of Derceto in Phœnicia, and a wonderful sight it is; one half is a woman, but the part which extends from the thighs to the feet ends in a fish's tail.[26] The effigy, however, which is at Hierapolis is a complete woman.[27] The reasons for this story are plain to understand; they deem fishes holy objects,[28] and never touch them, while of birds they use all but pigeons for food; the pigeon is in their eyes sacred.[29] It appears to them then that what we have described was done in honour of Derceto and Semiramis. The former, because Derceto has the form of a fish; the latter, because the lower half of Semiramis takes the form of a pigeon. I, however, should probably conclude that the temple in question belongs to Semiramis; that the shrine is Derceto's I can in no wise believe, since even amongst the Egyptians there are some who will not touch fish as food, and they certainly do not observe this restriction in favour of Derceto.

15. There is, however, another sacred story which I had from the lips of a wise man—that the goddess was Rhea, and the shrine the work of Attes. Now this Attes was by nation a Lydian, and he first taught the mysteries of Rhea.[30] The ritual of the Phrygians and the Lydians and the Samothracians was entirely learnt from Attes.

Ramsay in support of his contention that the poor quality of the fish was the underlying cause of this apparent "totemic prohibition." But see Dussaud, *Rev. Arch.*, 1904, ii. 247. See also Belin de Ballu, in his *Œuvres de Lucien* (Paris, 1789), p. 149, note 2. Ancient superstitions and uses are recited by Pliny, *Nat. Hist.* xxxii. 16.

29. See § 54 and note 65.

30. RHEA.—Not the Cretan goddess (Diod. v. 66), but Kybele, with whom the Greeks settled in Asia Minor identified her (Strabo, x. iii. 15; Farnell, Cults, iii. vi.). For the Minoan goddess, see especially Evans, *The Palace of Knossos*, Annual British School at Athens (1900-1901), pp. 29, 30; and his *Mykenæan Tree and Pillar Cult*, § 22. On the cult of the goddess in Asia Minor, see especially Ramsay, in numerous works (Bibl. *L. H.*, pp. 393-4), *e.g.*, *Jour. R. Asiatic Soc.*, 1883, and in Hastings' *Dict. Bib.*, extra vol., p. 122 *ff.* The points of resemblance to Atargatis, and the relationship of both with the Hittite goddess, are discussed in our Introduction, pp. 20, 26, and note 69. (*Cf.* also Farnell, *Greece and Babylon*, pp. 62-63.) On the cult transferred to Italy, see Cumont, *Oriental Relig. in Rom. Pag.*, 1911, p. 46 *ff.*, and our Illustration, Fig. 8, p. 73.

ὡς γάρ μιν ἡ Ῥέη ἔτεμεν, βίου μὲν ἀνδρηίου ἀπεπαύσατο, μορφὴν δὲ θηλέην ἠμείψατο καὶ ἐσθῆτα γυναικηίην ἐνεδύσατο καὶ ἐς πᾶσαν γῆν φοιτέων ὄργιά τε ἐπετέλεεν καὶ τὰ ἔπαθεν ἀπηγέετο καὶ Ῥέην ἤειδεν. ἐν τοῖσιν καὶ ἐς Συρίην ἀπίκετο. ὡς δὲ οἱ πέρην Εὐφρήτεω ἄνθρωποι οὔτε αὐτὸν οὔτε ὄργια ἐδέκοντο, ἐν τῷδε τῷ χώρῳ τὸ ἱρὸν ἐποιήσατο. σημήια δέ· ἡ θεὸς τὰ πολλὰ ἐς Ῥέην ἐπικνέεται. λέοντες γάρ μιν φέρουσι καὶ τύμπανον ἔχει καὶ ἐπὶ τῇ κεφαλῇ πυργοφορέει, ὁκοίην Ῥέην Λυδοὶ ποιέουσιν. ἔλεγεν δὲ καὶ Γάλλων πέρι, οἵ εἰσιν ἐν τῷ ἱρῷ, ὅτι Γάλλοι Ἥρῃ μὲν οὐδαμά, Ῥέῃ δὲ τέμνονται καὶ Ἄττεα μιμέονται.

[16] Τὰ δέ μοι εὐπρεπέα μὲν δοκέει ἔμμεναι, ἀληθέα δὲ οὔ· ἐπεὶ καὶ τῆς τομῆς ἄλλην αἰτίην ἤκουσα πολλὸν πιστοτέρην. ἁνδάνει δέ μοι ἃ λέγουσιν τοῦ ἱροῦ πέρι τοῖς Ἕλλησι τὰ πολλὰ ὁμολογέοντες, τὴν μὲν θεὸν Ἥρην δοκέοντες, τὸ δ' ἔργον Διονύσου τοῦ Σεμέλης ποίημα· καὶ γὰρ δὴ Διόνυσος ἐς Συρίην ἀπίκετο κείνην ὁδὸν τὴν ἦλθεν ἐς Αἰθιοπίην. καὶ ἔστι πολλὰ ἐν τῷ ἱρῷ Διονύσου ποιητέω σήματα, ἐν τοῖσι καὶ ἐσθῆτες βάρβαροι καὶ λίθοι Ἰνδοὶ καὶ ἐλεφάντων κέρεα, τὰ Διόνυσος ἐξ Αἰθιόπων ἤνεικεν, καὶ φαλλοὶ δὲ ἑστᾶσι ἐν τοῖσι προπυλαίοισι δύο κάρτα μεγάλοι, ἐπὶ τῶν ἐπίγραμμα τοιόνδε ἐπιγέγραπται,

---

31. See also §§ 27, 51. *Cf.* the legends that Dionysus received woman's clothes from Rhea at Cybela (Apollod. iii. v. 1); and that Hercules, having yielded up his weapons, including his axe, received woman's dress from Omphale (Ovid, *Fasti*, ii. 305 *ff*; Diodorus, iv. ii.; etc.).

32. It is instructive to note that the Mitannians, who occupied the eastern side of the Euphrates in the fifteenth and fourteenth centuries B.C., though in some way related to the Hittites, embraced ethnic elements whose deities were radically different, including the Vedic cycle, Mithras, Varuna, etc. *Cf.* Winckler, *Milted. d. Deut. Orient. Ges.*, No. 35 (Dec., 1907), p. 51 (transl. Williams, *Liv. Ann. Arch.*, iv. p. 93, Extract xxiv.). In post-Hittite times the increasing tendency to local development must have emphasised the distinction between the Assyrian and the Phrygian conceptions of the goddess.

33. *Cf.* § 32, etc., where Lucian states that she holds a sceptre in one hand and a distaff in the other, and illustration, p. 72. The "tower on her head,"

For when Rhea deprived him of his powers, he put off his manly garb and assumed the appearance of a woman and her dress,[31] and roaming over the whole earth he performed his mysterious rites, narrating his sufferings and chanting the praises of Rhea. In the course of his wanderings he passed also into Syria. Now, when the men from beyond Euphrates would neither receive him nor his mysteries,[32] he reared a temple to himself on this very spot. The tokens of this fact are as follows: She is drawn by lions, she holds a drum in her hand and carries a tower on her head, just as the Lydians make Rhea to do.[33] He also affirmed that the Galli who are in the temple in no case castrate themselves in honour of Juno, but of Rhea, and this in imitation of Attes.

16. All this seems to me more specious than true, for I have heard a different and more credible reason given for their castration. I approve of the remarks about the temple made by those who in the main accept the theories of the Greeks: according to these the goddess is Hera, but the work was carried out by Dionysus,[34] the son of Semele: Dionysus visited Syria on his journey to Aethiopia. There are in the temple many tokens that Dionysus was its actual founder: for instance, barbaric raiment, Indian precious stones, and elephants' tusks brought by Dionysus from the Aethiopians. Further, a pair of phalli of great size are seen standing in the vestibule, bearing the inscription,

---

i.e., mural crown, emblematic of the goddess as protectress of her cities, is an invariable feature on all but the latest coins, where it sometimes degenerates (see Frontispiece, Nos. 1, 8). Compare the chief Hittite goddess (see Fig. 1), and Kybele or Rhea (Fig. 8, p. 73), who is described as *turrita* by Lucretius.

34. *Cf.* Diod., iv. (i.). On the cult of Dionysus, *cf.* Farnell, *Cults*, v. His legends, rites and mysteries largely borrowed from Asia Minor (Furtwängler in Roscher's *Lexikon*). Identified with Attis and Adonis by Socrates and Plutarch; and with Osiris also by Herodotus (*cf.* Frazer, *op. cit.*, p. 357). Macrobius recognises all four as sun-gods.

On the further reference to mannikins, see Hartmann, "Ein Phallobates," in *Jahrbuch d. K. Deut. Archä. Inst.*, xxvii., 1912 (i.), p. 54. For this reference we are indebted to Professor Bosanquet. Dragendorff seems to us to rightly doubt this writer's chief inference (*loc. cit.* in an editorial note at the end).

"τούσδε φαλλοὺς Διόνυσος Ἥρῃ μητρυιῇ ἀνέθηκα.» τὸ ἐμοὶ μέν νυν καὶ τόδε ἀρκέει, ἐρέω δὲ καὶ ἄλλ' ὅ τι ἐστὶν ἐν τῷ νηῷ Διονύσου ὄργιον. φαλλοὺς Ἕλληνες Διονύσῳ ἐγείρουσιν, ἐπὶ τῶν καὶ τοιόνδε τι φέρουσιν, ἄνδρας μικροὺς ἐκ ξύλου πεποιημένους, μεγάλα αἰδοῖα ἔχοντας· καλέεται δὲ τάδε νευρόσπαστα. ἔστι δὲ καὶ τόδε ἐν τῷ ἱρῷ· ἐν δεξιῇ τοῦ νηοῦ κάθηται μικρὸς ἀνὴρ χάλκεος ἔχων αἰδοῖον μέγα.

17. Τοσάδε μὲν ἀμφὶ τῶν οἰκιστέων τοῦ ἱροῦ μυθολογέουσιν. ἤδη δὲ ἐρέω καὶ τοῦ νηοῦ πέρι θέσιός τε ὅκως ἐγένετο καὶ ὅστις μιν ἐποιήσατο. λέγουσι τὸν νηὸν τὸν νῦν ἐόντα μὴ ἔμμεναι τὸν τὴν ἀρχὴν γεγενημένον, ἀλλ' ἐκεῖνον μὲν κατενεχθῆναι χρόνῳ ὕστερον, τὸν δὲ νῦν ἐόντα Στρατονίκης ἔμμεναι ποίημα, γυναικὸς τοῦ Ἀσσυρίων βασιλέως.

Δοκέει δέ μοι ἡ Στρατονίκη ἐκείνη ἔμμεναι, τῆς ὁ πρόγονος ἠρήσατο, τὸν ἤλεγξεν τοῦ ἰητροῦ ἐπινοίη· ὡς γάρ μιν ἡ συμφορὴ κατέλαβεν, ἀμηχανέων τῷ κακῷ αἰσχρῷ δοκέοντι κατ' ἡσυχίην ἐνόσεεν, ἔκειτο δὲ ἀλγέων οὐδέν, καί οἱ ἥ τε χροιὴ πάμπαν ἐτρέπετο καὶ τὸ σῶμα δι' ἡμέρης ἐμαραίνετο. ὁ δὲ ἰητρὸς ὡς εἶδέ μιν ἐς οὐδὲν ἐμφανὲς ἀρρωστέοντα, ἔγνω τὴν νοῦσον ἔρωτα ἔμμεναι. ἔρωτος δὲ ἀφανέος πολλὰ σημήια, ὀφθαλμοί τε ἀσθενέες καὶ φωνὴ καὶ χροιὴ καὶ δάκρυα. μαθὼν δὲ ταῦτα ἐποίεε· χειρὶ μὲν τῇ δεξιῇ εἶχε τοῦ νεηνίσκου τὴν καρδίην, ἐκάλεε δὲ τοὺς ἀνὰ τὴν οἰκίην πάντας· ὁ δὲ τῶν μὲν ἄλλων ἐσιόντων πάντων ἐν ἠρεμίῃ μεγάλῃ ἦν, ὡς δὲ ἡ μητρυιὴ ἀπίκετο, τήν τε χροιὴν ἠλλάξατο καὶ ἰδρώειν ἄρξατο

---

35. The stories of Stratonice and of Combabus which follow, §§ 17-25, are not of special interest. They seem to include garbled local details from the legends of Istar and Tammuz, and to be introduced as the fulfilment of Lucian's wish to explain the origin of emasculation and other customs among the Galli (see end of § 15). None the less, Stratonice is a recognisable historical character, wife of Seleucus Nicator (of Antioch), at the close of the third century B.C., and Movers (i., p. 687) has urged the identity of Combabus with the god of

On the Syrian Goddess 53

"I, Dionysus, dedicated these phalli to Hera my stepmother." This proof satisfies me. And I will describe another curiosity to be found in this temple, a sacred symbol of Dionysus. The Greeks erect phalli in honour of Dionysus, and on these they carry, singular to say, mannikins made of wood, with enormous pudenda; they call these puppets. There is this further curiosity in the temple: as you enter, on the right hand, a small brazen statue meets your eye of a man in a sitting posture, with parts of monstrous size.

17. These are the legends concerning the founders of the temple. I will proceed to speak of the edifice itself and its position: how it was built and who built it. They affirm that the temple as it exists now is not that which was built originally: the primitive temple fell to pieces in the course of time: the present one they say was the work of Stratonice, the wife of the king of the Assyrians.[35]

This I take to be the Stratonice of whom her stepson was enamoured, and the skill of a doctor detected the intrigue: for the lover, overpowered by the malady of his passion, bewildered by the thought of his shameful caprice, lay sick in silence. He lay sick, and though no ache was in any limb, yet his colour was gone, and his frame was growing frailer day by day. The doctor, seeing that he was suffering from no definite disease, perceived that his malady was none other than love. Many are the symptoms of secret love: languor of vision, change in the voice and complexion, and frequent tears. The doctor, aware of this, acted as follows: he laid his hand on the heart of the young man, and summoned all the domestics in the household. The patient remained tranquil and unmoved on the entrance of the rest, but when his stepmother came in he grew pale and fell to sweating and trembling,

---

Hierapolis. On the resemblance of the name to the Elamite *Khumbaba*, *cf.* Ungnad, *D. Gilgamesch-Epos*, p. 77, n. For this reference we are indebted to Professor Lehmann-Haupt. Six (*Num. Chron.*, 1878, p. 117) explains the main feature of Lucian's story in these words: ". . . la reine se fit initier aux actes religieux; et prit part aux cérémonies que célébraient les Syriens en l'honneur de leur déesse."

καὶ τρόμῳ εἴχετο καὶ ἡ καρδίη ἀνεπάλλετο. τὰ δὲ γιγνόμενα ἐμφανέα τῷ ἰητρῷ τὸν ἔρωτα ἐποίεεν, καί μιν ὧδε ἰήσατο.

18. καλέσας τοῦ νεηνίσκου τὸν πατέρα κάρτα ὀρρωδέοντα, «Ἥδε ἡ νοῦσος,» ἔφη, «ἣν ὁ παῖς ὅδε ἀρρωστέει, οὐ νοῦσός ἐστιν, ἀλλὰ ἀδικίη· ὅδε γάρ τοι ἀλγέει μὲν οὐδέν, ἔρως δέ μιν καὶ φρενοβλαβείη ἔχει. ἐπιθυμέει δὲ τῶν οὐδαμὰ τεύξεται, φιλέων γυναῖκα ἐμήν, τὴν ἐγὼ οὔτι μετήσομαι.» ὁ μὲν ὢν τοιάδε σοφίῃ ἐψεύδετο. ὁ δὲ αὐτίκα ἐλίσσετο, «Πρός τε σοφίης καὶ ἰητρικῆς, μή μοι παῖδα ὀλέσῃς· οὐ γὰρ ἐθέλων ταύτῃ συμφορῇ ἔσχετο, ἀλλὰ οἱ ἡ νοῦσος ἀεκουσίη. τῷ σὺ μηδαμὰ ζηλοτυπέων πένθος ἐγεῖραι πάσῃ βασιληίῃ μηδὲ ἰητρὸς ἐὼν φόνον προξενέειν ἰητρικῇ.» ὁ μὲν ὧδε ἀγνὼς ἐὼν ἐδέετο. ὁ δέ μιν αὖτις ἀμείβετο, «Ἀνόσια σπεύδεις γάμον ἐμὸν ἀπαιρεόμενος ἠδὲ ἰητρὸν ἄνδρα βιώμενος. σὺ δὲ κῶς ἂν αὐτὸς ἔπρηξας, εἴ τοι σὴν γυναῖκα ἐπόθεεν, ἐμεῦ τάδε δεόμενος;» ὁ δὲ πρὸς τάδε ἔλεγεν ὡς οὐδ᾿ αὐτὸς ἄν κοτε γυναικὸς ἐφείσατο οὐδὲ παιδὶ σωτηρίης ἐφθόνεεν, εἰ καί τι μητρυιῆς ἐπεθύμεεν· οὐ γὰρ ὁμοίην συμφορὴν ἔμμεναι γαμετὴν ἢ παῖδα ὀλέσαι. ὡς δὲ τάδε ὁ ἰητρὸς ἤκουσεν, «Τί τοι,» ἔφη, «ἐμὲ λίσσεαι; καὶ γάρ τοι σὴν γυναῖκα ποθέει· τὰ δὲ ἐγὼ ἔλεγον πάντα ἔην ψεύδεα.» πείθεται μὲν τουτέοισι, καὶ τῷ μὲν παιδὶ λείπει καὶ γυναῖκα καὶ βασιληίην, αὐτὸς δὲ ἐς τὴν Βαβυλωνίην χώρην ἀπίκετο καὶ πόλιν ἐπὶ τῷ Εὐφρήτῃ ἐπώνυμον ἑωυτοῦ ἐποιήσατο, ἔνθα οἱ καὶ ἡ τελευτὴ ἐγένετο. ὧδε μὲν ὁ ἰητρὸς ἔρωτα ἔγνω τε καὶ ἰήσατο.

[19] Ἥδε δὴ ὦν ἡ Στρατονίκη ἔτι τῷ προτέρῳ ἀνδρὶ συνοικέουσα ὄναρ τοιόνδε ἐθεήσατο, ὥς μιν ἡ Ἥρη ἐκέλευεν ἐγεῖραί οἱ τὸν ἐν τῇ ἱρῇ πόλει νηόν, εἰ δὲ ἀπειθέοι, πολλά οἱ καὶ κακὰ ἀπείλεεν. ἡ δὲ τὰ μὲν πρῶτα οὐδεμίαν ὤρην ἐποιέετο· μετὰ δέ, ὥς μιν μεγάλη νοῦσος ἔλαβεν, τῷ τε ἀνδρὶ τὴν ὄψιν ἀπηγήσατο καὶ τὴν Ἥρην ἱλάσκετο καὶ στήσειν τὸν νηὸν ὑπεδέξατο. καὶ αὐτίκα ὑγιέα γενομένην

and his heart beat violently. These symptoms betrayed his passion to the doctor, who cured him in the following way.

18. Summoning the young man's father, who was racked by anxiety, he explained to him that the young man's malady was no normal malady, but a wrongful action: "he has no painful symptoms; he is possessed by love and madness. He longs to possess what he will never obtain; he loves my wife, whom I will never give up." This was the trick of the wise physician. The father straightway begged the doctor by his prudence and professional skill not to let his son perish. "His malady depended not on his will; it was involuntary. Pray then do not you let your jealousy bring grief on the whole realm, and do not, dear doctor, draw unpopularity on your profession." Such was the unwitting father's request. The doctor replied: "Your request is scandalous. You would deprive me of my wife and outrage the honour of a medical man. I put it to you, what would be your conduct, since you are deprecating mine, if your wife were the object of his guilty love?" He replied that he would not spare his own wife nor would he begrudge his son his life, even though that son were enamoured of his own stepmother: losing one's wife was a less misfortune than losing one's son. The doctor on hearing this said: "Why then offer me these entreaties? In good truth, your wife is the object of his love. What I said to you was all a made-up story." The father followed this advice, and handed over his wife and his kingdom to his son, and he himself departed into the region of Babylonia and founded a city on the Euphrates which bore his name: and there he died. Thus it was that our wise doctor detected and cured the malady.

19. Now this Stratonice, when still married to her former husband, saw in a vision Hera exhorting her to rear a temple to this goddess at Hierapolis. Should she neglect to obey, she was menaced by the goddess with manifold evils. The queen began by disregarding the dream, but later, when seized by a dangerous illness, she told the vision to her husband, and appeased Hera, and undertook to raise the temple. Hardly had she recovered

ὁ ἀνὴρ ἐς τὴν ἱρὴν πόλιν ἔπεμπε, σὺν δὲ οἱ καὶ χρήματα καὶ στρατιὴν πολλήν, τοὺς μὲν οἰκοδομέειν, τοὺς δὲ καὶ τοῦ ἀσφαλέος εἵνεκα. καλέσας δέ τινα τῶν ἑωυτοῦ φίλων, νεηνίην κάρτα καλόν, τῷ οὔνομα ἦν Κομβάβος, «Ἐγώ τοι,» ἔφη, «ὦ Κομβάβε, ἐσθλὸν ἐόντα φιλέω τε μάλιστα φίλων ἐμῶν καὶ πάμπαν ἐπαινέω σοφίης τε καὶ εὐνοίης τῆς ἐς ἡμέας, ἣν δὴ ἐπεδέξαο. νῦν δέ μοι χρειὼ μεγάλης πίστιος, τῷ σε θέλω γυναικὶ ἐμῇ ἑσπόμενον ἔργον τέ μοι ἐπιτελέσαι καὶ ἱρὰ τελέσαι καὶ στρατιῆς ἐπικρατέειν· σοὶ δὲ ἀπικομένῳ ἐξ ἡμέων τιμὴ μεγάλη ἔσσεται.»

Πρὸς τάδε ὁ Κομβάβος αὐτίκα λίσσετο πολλὰ λιπαρέων μή μιν ἐκπέμπειν μηδὲ πιστεύειν οἱ τὰ πολλὸν ἑωυτοῦ μέζονα χρήματα καὶ γυναῖκα καὶ ἔργον ἱρόν. τὰ δὲ ὀρρώδεεν μή κοτέ οἱ ζηλοτυπίη χρόνῳ ὑστέρῳ ἐς τὴν Στρατονίκην γένοιτο, τὴν μοῦνος ἀπάξειν ἔμελλεν.

[20] ὡς δὲ οὐδαμὰ ἐπείθετο, ὁ δὲ ἱκεσίης δευτέρης ἅπτεται δοῦναί οἱ χρόνον ἑπτὰ ἡμερέων, μετὰ δὲ ἀποστεῖλαί μιν τελέσαντά τι τῶν μάλιστα ἐδέετο. τυχὼν δὲ ῥηιδίως, ἐς τὸν ἑωυτοῦ οἶκον ἀπικνέεται καὶ πεσὼν χαμᾶζε τοιάδε ὠδύρετο· "Ὦ δείλαιος, τί μοι ταύτης τῆς πίστιος; τί δέ μοι ὁδοῦ, τῆς τέλος ἤδη δέρκομαι; νέος μὲν ἐγὼ καὶ γυναικὶ καλῇ ἕψομαι. τὸ δέ μοι μεγάλη συμφορὴ ἔσσεται, εἰ μὴ ἔγωγε πᾶσαν αἰτίην κακοῦ ἀποθήσομαι· τῷ με χρῆν μέγα ἔργον ἀποτελέσαι, τό μοι πάντα φόβον ἰήσεται.»

Τάδε εἰπὼν ἀτελέα ἑωυτὸν ἐποίεεν, καὶ ταμὼν τὰ αἰδοῖα ἐς ἀγγήιον μικρὸν κατέθετο σμύρνῃ τε ἅμα καὶ μέλιτι καὶ ἄλλοισι θυώμασι· καὶ ἔπειτα σφρηγῖδι τὴν ἐφόρεε σημηνάμενος τὸ τρῶμα ἰῆτο. μετὰ δέ, ὥς μιν ὁδοιπορέειν ἐδόκεεν, ἀπικόμενος ἐς τὸν βασιλέα πολλῶν παρεόντων διδοῖ τε ἅμα τὸ ἀγγήιον καὶ λέγει ὧδε· "Ὦ δέσποτα, τόδε μοι μέγα κειμήλιον ἐν τοῖσι οἰκείοισι ἀπεκέατο, τὸ ἐγὼ κάρτα ἐπόθεον·

when she was despatched by her husband to Hierapolis, and a large sum of money with her, and a large army too, partly to aid in the building operations and partly to ensure her safety. He summoned one of her friends called Combabus, a young man of handsome presence, and said, "Combabus, I know thee for an honest man, and of all my friends I love thee best, and I commend thee greatly alike for thy wisdom and for thy goodwill which thou hast shown to us. At the present moment I have need of all thy confidence, and thus I wish thee to accompany my wife, and to carry out my work, and to perform the sacrifices due, and to command my army. On my return great honour shall fall to thee."

Combabus begged and prayed not to be despatched, and not to be entrusted with matters far above his powers—moneys, the lady, the holy work: not merely so, but he feared lest in the future some jealousy might make itself felt as to his relations with Stratonice, as he was unaccompanied should he consent to escort her.

20. The king, however, refused to be moved; so Combabus prayed as an alternative that a respite of seven days might be granted him: after that interval he was willing to be despatched after attending to his immediate needs. On obtaining this respite, which was willingly granted, he departed to his house, and throwing himself on the ground, he thus deplored his lot: "Unhappy me! Why this confidence in myself? To what end is this journey, whose results I already see? I am young and the lady whom I escort is fair. This will prove a great and mighty disaster, unless I remove entirely the cause of the evil. Thus I must even perform a mighty deed which will heal all my fears."

Saying this he unmanned himself, and he stowed away the mutilated pudenda in a little vessel together with myrrh and honey and spices of various sorts. He sealed this vessel up with a ring which he wore; and finally he proceeded to dress his wound. As soon as he deemed himself fit to travel he made his way to the king, and before a large company reached the vessel forth and spoke as follows: "Master! This my most precious treasure was stored up in my house, and I loved it well:

νῦν δὲ ἐπεὶ μεγάλην ὁδὸν ἔρχομαι, παρὰ σοὶ τόδε θήσομαι. σὺ δέ μοι ἀσφαλέως ἔχειν· τόδε γάρ μοι χρυσοῦ βέλτερον, τόδε μοι ψυχῆς ἐμῆς ἀντάξιον. εὖτ᾽ ἂν δὲ ἀπίκωμαι, σόον αὖτις ἀποίσομαι.» ὁ δὲ δεξάμενος ἑτέρῃ σφρηγῖδι ἐσημαίνετο καὶ τοῖσι ταμίῃσι φρουρέειν ἐνετείλατο.

[21] Κομβάβος μέν νυν τὸ ἀπὸ τοῦδε ἀσφαλέα ὁδὸν ἤνυεν· ἀπικόμενοι δὲ ἐς τὴν ἱρὴν πόλιν σπουδῇ τὸν νηὸν οἰκοδόμεον καὶ σφίσι τρία ἔτεα ἐν τῷ ἔργῳ ἐξεγένετο, ἐν τοῖσι ἀπέβαινε τάπερ ὁ Κομβάβος ὀρρώδεεν. ἡ Στρατονίκη γὰρ χρόνον ἐπὶ πολλὸν συνόντα μιν ποθέειν ἄρχετο, μετὰ δέ οἱ καὶ κάρτα ἐπεμήνατο. καὶ λέγουσιν οἱ ἐν τῇ ἱρῇ πόλει τὴν Ἥρην τουτέων αἰτίην ἐθέλουσαν γενέσθαι, Κομβάβον ἐσθλὸν μὲν ἐόντα λαθέειν μηδαμά, Στρατονίκην δὲ τίσασθαι, ὅτι οὐ ῥηιδίως τὸν νηὸν ὑπέσχετο.

[22] Ἡ δὲ τὰ μὲν πρῶτα ἐσωφρόνεεν καὶ τὴν νοῦσον ἔκρυπτεν· ὡς δέ οἱ τὸ κακὸν μέζον ἡσυχίης ἐγένετο, ἐς ἐμφανὲς ἐτρύχετο κλαίεσκέν τε δι᾽ ἡμέρης καὶ Κομβάβον ἀνεκαλέετο καί οἱ πάντα Κομβάβος ἦν. τέλος δὲ ἀμηχανέουσα τῇ συμφορῇ εὐπρεπέα ἱκεσίην ἐδίζητο. ἄλλῳ μὲν ὦν τὸν ἔρωτα ὁμολογέειν ἐφυλάσσετο, αὐτὴ δὲ ἐπιχειρέειν αἰδέετο. ἐπινοέει ὦν τοιάδε, οἴνῳ ἑωυτὴν μεθύσασα ἐς λόγους οἱ ἐλθεῖν. ἅμα δὲ οἴνῳ ἐσιόντι παρρησίη τε ἐσέρχεται καὶ ἡ ἀποτυχίη οὐ κάρτα αἰσχρή, ἀλλὰ τῶν πρησσομένων ἕκαστα ἐς ἀγνοίην ἀναχωρέει.

Ὡς δέ οἱ ἐδόκεε, καὶ ἐποίεε ταῦτα. καὶ ἐπεὶ ἐκ δείπνου ἐγένοντο, ἀπικομένη ἐς τὰ οἰκεῖα ἐν τοῖσι Κομβάβος αὐλίζετο, λίσσετό τε καὶ γούνων ἅπτετο καὶ τὸν ἔρωτα ὡμολόγεεν. ὁ δὲ τόν τε λόγον ἀπηνέως ἀπεδέκετο καὶ τὸ ἔργον ἀναίνετο καί οἱ τὴν μέθην ἐπεκάλεεν. ἀπειλούσης δὲ μέγα τι κακὸν ἑωυτὴν ἐργάσασθαι, δείσας πάντα οἱ λόγον ἔφηνεν καὶ πᾶσαν τὴν ἑωυτοῦ πάθην ἀπηγήσατο καὶ τὸ ἔργον ἐς ἐμφανὲς ἤνεικεν. ἰδοῦσα δὲ ἡ Στρατονίκη τὰ οὔποτε ἔλπετο, μανίης μὲν ἐκείνης ἔσχετο, ἔρωτος δὲ οὐδαμὰ ἐλήθετο,

but now that I am entering on a long journey, I will set it in thy keeping. Do thou keep it well: for it is dearer to me than gold and more precious to me than life. On my return I shall receive it again." The king was pleased to receive the vessel, and after sealing it with another seal he entrusted it to his treasurers to keep.

21. So Combabus from this time forth continued his journey in peace. Arrived at Hierapolis they built the temple with all diligence, and three years passed while they were at their task. Meantime the event came to pass which Combabus had feared. Stratonice began to love him who had been her companion for so long a time: her love passed into an overpowering passion. Those of Hierapolis affirm that Hera was the willing cause of this trouble: she knew full well that Combabus was an upright man, but she wished to wreak her wrath on Stratonice for her unwillingness to undertake the building of the temple.

22. The queen was at first coy and tried to hide her passion, but when her trouble left her no longer any repose, she openly displayed her irritation and wept the whole day long, and called out repeatedly for Combabus: Combabus was everything to her. At last, in despair at her impotency to master her passion, she sought a suitable occasion for supplicating his love. She was too cautious to admit her passion to a stranger, but her modesty prevented her from facing the situation. Finally she hits on this plan; that she should confront him after she should have drunk deeply of wine; for courage rises after drinking and a repulse seems then less degrading, and actions performed under the influence of wine are set down to ignorance.

Thus she acted as she thought best. After supper she entered the chamber in which Combabus dwelt, and besought him, embracing his knees, and she avowed her guilty love. He heard her words with disgust and rejected her advances, reproaching her with drunkenness. She, however, threatened that she would bring on him a great calamity; on which he trembled, and he told her all his story and narrated all that he had done and finally disclosed to her the manifest proofs of his statement. When the queen witnessed this unexpected proof her passion indeed was quenched,

ἀλλὰ πάντα οἱ συνεοῦσα ταύτην παραμυθίην ἐποιέετο ἔρωτος ἀπρήκτοιο. ἔστιν ὁ ἔρως οὗτος ἐν τῇ ἱρῇ πόλει καὶ ἔτι νῦν γίγνεται· γυναῖκες Γάλλων ἐπιθυμέουσι καὶ γυναιξὶ Γάλλοι ἐπιμαίνονται, ζηλοτυπέει δὲ οὐδείς, ἀλλὰ σφίσι τὸ χρῆμα κάρτα ἱρὸν νομίζουσιν.

23. Τὰ δ' ὦν ἐν τῇ ἱρῇ πόλει ἀμφὶ τὴν Στρατονίκην οὐδαμὰ τὸν βασιλέα λέληθεν, ἀλλὰ πολλοὶ ἀπικνεόμενοι κατηγόρεον καὶ τὰ γιγνόμενα ἀπηγέοντο. ἐπὶ τοῖσι περιαλγέων ἐξ ἀτελέος τοῦ ἔργου Κομβάβον μετεκάλεεν. ἄλλοι δὲ λέγουσι λόγον οὔτι ἀληθέα, τὴν Στρατονίκην, ἐπειδὴ ἀπέτυχε τῶν ἐδέετο, αὐτὴν γράψασαν ἐς τὸν ἄνδρα τοῦ Κομβάβου κατηγορέειν πείρην οἱ ἐπικαλέουσαν, καὶ τὸ Ἕλληνες Σθενεβοίης πέρι λέγουσι καὶ Φαίδρης τῆς Κνωσσίης, ταυτὶ καὶ Ἀσσύριοι ἐς Στρατονίκην μυθολογέουσιν. ἐγὼ μέν νυν οὐδὲ Σθενεβοίην πείθομαι οὐδὲ Φαίδρην τοιάδε ἐπιτελέσαι, εἰ τὸν Ἱππόλυτον ἀτρεκέως ἐπόθεε Φαίδρη. ἀλλὰ τὰ μὲν ἐχέτω ὅκως καὶ ἐγένετο.

24. Ὡς δὲ ἡ ἀγγελίη ἐς τὴν ἱρὴν πόλιν ἀπίκετο ἔγνω τε ὁ Κομβάβος τὴν αἰτίην, θαρσέων τε ἦεν, ὅτι οἱ ἡ ἀπολογίη οἴκοι ἐλείπετο, καί μιν ἐλθόντα ὁ βασιλεὺς αὐτίκα μὲν ἔδησέν τε καὶ ἐν φρουρῇ εἶχεν· μετὰ δέ, παρεόντων οἱ τῶν φίλων οἳ καὶ τότε πεμπομένῳ τῷ Κομβάβῳ παρεγένοντο, παραγαγὼν ἐς μέσον κατηγορέειν ἄρχετο καί οἱ μοιχείην τε καὶ ἀκολασίην προὔφερεν· κάρτα δὲ δεινοπαθέων πίστιν τε καὶ φιλίην ἀνεκαλέετο, λέγων τρισσὰ Κομβάβον ἀδικέειν μοιχόν τε ἐόντα καὶ ἐς πίστιν ὑβρίσαντα καὶ ἐς θεὸν ἀσεβέοντα, τῆς ἐν τῷ ἔργῳ τοιάδε ἔπρηξεν. πολλοὶ δὲ παρεστεῶτες ἤλεγχον ὅτι ἀναφανδὸν σφέας ἀλλήλοισι συνεόντας εἶδον. πᾶσιν δὲ τέλος ἐδόκεεν αὐτίκα θνῄσκειν Κομβάβον θανάτου ἄξια ἐργασμένον.

but she never forgot her love, but in all her intercourse she cherished the solace of her unavailing affection. The memory of this love is still alive at Hierapolis and is maintained in this way; the women still are enamoured of the Galli, and the Galli again love the women with passion; but there is no jealousy at all, and this love passes among them for a holy passion.

23. The king was well informed about Stratonice's doings at Hierapolis, for many who came thence brought the tale of what was happening. The monarch was deeply moved by the tidings, and before the work was finished summoned Combabus to his presence. Others narrate with respect to this a circumstance wholly untrue; that Stratonice finding her prayers repulsed wrote with her own hand to her husband and accused Combabus of making an attempt upon her modesty; and what the Greeks allege about their Stheneboea and about Phaedra the Cnosian the Assyrians tell in the same way about Stratonice. For my part I do not believe that either Stheneboea nor Phaedra acted thus if Phaedra really loved Hippolytus. However, let the old version remain for what it is worth.

24. When, however, the news was brought to Hierapolis, Combabus took count of the charge and departed in a spirit of full confidence, conscious that the visible proof necessary for his defence had been left in the city his home. On his arrival the king immediately put him in prison under strict guard. Then in the presence of the friends of the accused who had been present when Combabus was commissioned to depart, the king summoned him into open court and began to accuse him of adultery and evil lust; and deeply moved, recounting the confidence he had reposed in his favourite and his long friendship, he arraigned Combabus on three distinct charges: first, that he was an adulterer, secondly, that he had broken his trust, finally, that he had blasphemed the goddess by acting thus while engaged in her service. Many of the bystanders bore witness against him, saying that they had seen the guilty pair embracing. It was finally agreed that Combabus was worthy of death as his evil deeds had merited.

25. Ὁ δὲ τέως μὲν ἑστήκεεν λέγων οὐδέν· ἐπεὶ δὲ ἤδη ἐς τὸν φόνον ἤγετο, φθέγξατό τε καὶ τὸ κειμήλιον αἴτεε, λέγων ὡς ἀναιρέει μιν οὐχ ὕβριος οὐδὲ γάμων εἵνεκα, ἀλλὰ ἐκείνων ἐπιθυμέων τά οἱ ἀπιὼν παρεθήκατο. πρὸς τάδε ὁ βασιλεὺς καλέσας τὸν ταμίην ἐκέλευεν ἐνεῖκαι τά οἱ φρουρέειν ἔδωκεν· ὡς δὲ ἤνεικεν, λύσας τὴν σφρηγῖδα ὁ Κομβάβος τά τε ἐνεόντα ἐπέδειξεν καὶ ἑωυτὸν ὁκοῖα ἐπεπόνθεεν, ἔλεξέ τε, "Ὦ βασιλεῦ, τάδε τοι ἐγὼ ὀρρωδέων, εὖτέ με ταύτην ὁδὸν ἔπεμπες, ἀέκων ᾖον· καὶ ἐπεί με ἀναγκαίη μεγάλη ἐκ σέο κατέλαβεν, τοιάδε ἐπετέλεσα, ἐσθλὰ μὲν ἐς δεσπότεα, ἐμοὶ δὲ οὐκ εὐτυχέα. τοιόσδε μέντοι ἐὼν ἀνδρὸς ἐπ' ἀδικίην ἐγκαλέομαι."

Ὁ δὲ πρὸς τάδε ἀμβώσας περιέβαλέν τέ μιν καὶ δακρύων ἅμα ἔλεγεν, "Ὦ Κομβάβε, τί μέγα κακὸν εἰργάσαο; τί δὲ σεωυτὸν οὕτως ἀεικέλιον ἔργον μοῦνος ἀνδρῶν ἔπρηξας; τὰ οὐ πάμπαν ἐπαινέω. ὦ σχέτλιε, ὃς τοιάδε ἔτλης, οἷα μήτε σὲ παθέειν μήτ' ἐμὲ ἰδέσθαι ὤφελεν· οὐ γάρ μοι ταύτης ἀπολογίης ἔδεεν. ἀλλ' ἐπεὶ δαίμων τοιάδε ἤθελεν, πρῶτα μέν σοι τίσις ἐξ ἡμέων ἔσσεται, αὐτέων συκοφαντέων ὁ θάνατος, μετὰ δὲ μεγάλη δωρεὴ ἀπίξεται χρυσός τε πολλὸς καὶ ἄργυρος ἄπλετος καὶ ἐσθῆτες Ἀσσύριαι καὶ ἵπποι βασιλήιοι. ἀπίξεαι δὲ παρ' ἡμέας ἄνευ ἐσαγγελέος οὐδέ τις ἀπέρξει σε ἡμετέρης ὄψιος, οὐδ' ἢν γυναικὶ ἅμα εὐνάζωμαι." τάδε εἶπέν τε ἅμα καὶ ἐποίεεν· καὶ οἱ μὲν αὐτίκα ἐς φόνον ἤγοντο, τῷ δὲ τὰ δῶρα ἐδέδοτο καὶ ἡ φιλίη μέζων ἐγεγόνεεν. ἐδόκεεν δὲ οὐδεὶς ἔτι Ἀσσυρίων Κομβάβῳ σοφίην καὶ εὐδαιμονίην εἴκελος.

26. Μετὰ δὲ αἰτησάμενος ἐκτελέσαι τὰ λείποντα τῷ νηῷ—ἀτελέα γάρ μιν ἀπολελοίπεεν—αὖτις ἐπέμπετο, καὶ τόν τε νηὸν ἐξετέλεσε καὶ τὸ λοιπὸν αὐτοῦ ἔμενεν. ἔδωκεν δέ οἱ βασιλεὺς ἀρετῆς τε καὶ εὐεργεσίης εἵνεκα

25. He had stood up to this point in silence, but as he was being led to his fate, he spoke out, and demanded the restoration of his pledge, affirming that he was to be killed not for rebellious conduct against his king, nor for any violation of the king's married life, but solely because of the king's eagerness to possess what he had deposited at the royal court at his departure. The king thereon summoned his treasurer and bade him bring forth what he had committed to his custody. On its production, Combabus removed the seal and displayed the contents of the vessel, and showed how he himself had suffered thereby; adding, "This is just what I feared, O King, when thou didst send me on that errand: I left with a heavy heart, and I did my duty, constrained by sheer necessity. I obeyed my lord and master to mine own undoing. Such as I am, I stand accused of a crime which none but a man in every sense could have committed."

The king cried out in amazement at these words, embraced Combabus and said with tears, "What great ruin, Combabus, hast thou wrought upon thyself? What monstrous deed of ill hast thou, alone of men, wrought to thy sorrow? I cannot praise thee, rash spirit, for enduring to suffer this outrage; would that thou hadst never borne it; would that I had never seen its proofs! I needed not this thy defence. But since the deity hath willed it thus, I will grant thee, first and foremost, as thy revenge, the death of the informers: and next there shall follow a mighty gift, a store of silver and countless gold, and raiment of Assyria, and steeds from the royal stud. Thou shalt enter freely to us unannounced and none shall withstand thee: none shall keep thee from my sight, even were I by my wife's side." Thus he spake, and thus he acted; the informers were led off straightway to their execution; Combabus was laden with gifts, and the king's attachment to him was increased. No one of the Assyrians was deemed equal in wisdom and in fortune to Combabus.

26. On his request that he might complete what was unfinished in the construction of the temple—for he had left it unfinished—he was despatched anew; and he completed the temple, and there he abode. To mark his sense of the virtue and good deeds

ἐν τῷ ἱρῷ ἑστάναι χάλκεον· καὶ ἔτι ἐς τιμὴν ἐν τῷ ἱρῷ Κομβάβος χάλκεος, Ἑρμοκλέος τοῦ Ῥοδίου ποίημα, μορφὴν μὲν ὁκοίη γυνή, ἐσθῆτα δὲ ἀνδρηίην ἔχει.

Λέγεται δὲ τῶν φίλων τοὺς μάλιστά οἱ εὐνοέοντας ἐς παραμυθίην τοῦ πάθεος κοινωνίην ἑλέσθαι τῆς συμφορῆς· ἔτεμον γὰρ ἑωυτοὺς καὶ δίαιταν τὴν αὐτὴν ἐκείνῳ διαιτέοντο. ἄλλοι δὲ ἱρολογέουσιν ἐπὶ τῷ πρήγματι, λέγοντες ὡς ἡ Ἥρη φιλέουσα Κομβάβον πολλοῖσι τὴν τομὴν ἐπὶ νόον ἔβαλλεν, ὅκως μὴ μοῦνος ἐπὶ τῇ ἀνδρηίῃ λυπέοιτο.

[27] τὸ δὲ ἔθος τοῦτο ἐπειδὴ ἅπαξ ἐγένετο, ἔτι νῦν μένει· καὶ πολλοὶ ἑκάστου ἔτεος ἐν τῷ ἱρῷ τάμνονται καὶ θηλύνονται, εἴτε Κομβάβον παραμυθεόμενοι εἴτε καὶ Ἥρῃ χαρίζονται· τάμνονται δ' ὧν. ἐσθῆτα δὲ οἵδε οὐκέτι ἀνδρηίην ἔχουσιν, ἀλλὰ εἵματά τε γυναικήια φορέουσιν καὶ ἔργα γυναικῶν ἐπιτελέουσιν. ὡς δὲ ἐγὼ ἤκουον, ἀνακέαται καὶ τουτέων ἐς Κομβάβον ἡ αἰτίη· συνενείχθη γάρ οἱ καὶ τάδε. ξείνη γυνὴ ἐς πανήγυριν ἀπικομένη, ἰδοῦσα καλόν τε ἐόντα καὶ ἐσθῆτα ἔτι ἀνδρηίην ἔχοντα, ἔρωτι μεγάλῳ ἔσχετο, μετὰ δὲ μαθοῦσα ἀτελέα ἐόντα ἑωυτὴν διειργάσατο. ἐπὶ τοῖσι Κομβάβος, ἀθυμέων ὅτι οἱ ἀτυχέως τὰ ἐς Ἀφροδίτην ἔχει, ἐσθῆτα γυναικηίην ἐνεδύσατο, ὅκως μηκέτι ἑτέρη γυνὴ ἴσα ἐξαπατέοιτο. ἥδε αἰτίη Γάλλοισι στολῆς θηλέης. Κομβάβου μέν μοι τοσάδε εἰρήσθω, Γάλλων δὲ αὖτις ἐγὼ λόγῳ ὑστέρῳ μεμνήσομαι, τομῆς τε αὐτέων, ὅκως τάμνονται, καὶ ταφῆς ὁκοίην θάπτονται, καὶ ὅτευ εἵνεκα ἐς τὸ ἱρὸν οὐκ ἐσέρχονται· πρότερον δέ μοι θυμὸς εἰπεῖν θέσιός τε πέρι τοῦ νηοῦ καὶ μεγάθεος, καὶ δῆτα ἐρέω.

---

36. It would be inconsistent with what Lucian says in § 27 and elsewhere on the dress of the Galli to believe that this brazen statue really represented Combabus. His description suggests rather the figure of an Amazon.

of his architect, the king granted him a brazen statue of himself to stand in the temple of his construction. And even to the present day this brazen statue is seen standing in the temple, the work of Hermocles of Rhodes. Its form is that of a woman, but the garments are those of a man.³⁶

It is said, too, that his most intimate friends, as a proof of their sympathy, castrated themselves like him, and chose the same manner of life. Others there are who bring gods into the story and affirm that Combabus was beloved by Hera; and that it was she who inspired many with the idea of castrating themselves, so that her lover should not be the only one to lament the loss of his virility.

27. Meantime the custom once adopted remains even to-day, and many persons every year castrate themselves and lose their virile powers: whether it be out of sympathy with Combabus, or to find favour with Hera. They certainly castrate themselves, and then cease to wear man's garb; they don women's raiment and perform women's tasks.³⁷ I have heard the origin of this ascribed to Combabus as well, for the following event occurred to him. A certain foreign woman who had joined a sacred assembly, beholding a human form of extreme beauty and dressed in man's attire, became violently enamoured of him: after discovering that he was unsexed, she took away her life. Combabus accordingly in despair at his incapacity for love, donned woman's attire, that no woman in future might be deceived in the same way. This is the reason of the female attire of the Galli. Enough of Combabus and his story: in the course of my story I shall make mention of the Galli, and of their castration, and of the methods employed to effect it, and of the burial rites wherewith they are buried, and the reasons why they have no ingress to the temple; but before this I am inclined to speak of the site of the temple and of its size: and so I will even speak.

---

37. *Cf.* § 15 and, especially, § 51 below.

[28] Ὁ μὲν χῶρος αὐτός, ἐν τῷ τὸ ἱρὸν ἵδρυται, λόφος ἐστίν, κέαται δὲ κατὰ μέσον μάλιστα τῆς πόλιος, καί οἱ τείχεα δοιὰ περικέαται. τῶν δὲ τειχέων τὸ μὲν ἀρχαῖον, τὸ δὲ οὐ πολλὸν ἡμέων πρεσβύτερον. τὰ δὲ προπύλαια τοῦ ἱροῦ ἐς ἄνεμον βορέην ἀποκέκρινται, μέγαθος ὅσον τε ἑκατὸν ὀργυιέων. ἐν τούτοισι τοῖσι προπυλαίοισι καὶ οἱ φαλλοὶ ἑστᾶσι τοὺς Διόνυσος ἐστήσατο, ἡλικίην καὶ οἵδε τριηκοσίων ὀργυιέων. ἐς τουτέων τὸν ἕνα φαλλὸν ἀνὴρ ἑκάστου ἔτεος δὶς ἀνέρχεται οἰκέει τε ἐν ἄκρῳ τῷ φαλλῷ χρόνον ἑπτὰ ἡμερέων. αἰτίη δέ οἱ τῆς ἀνόδου ἥδε λέγεται. οἱ μὲν πολλοὶ νομίζουσιν ὅτι ὑψοῦ τοῖσι θεοῖσιν ὁμιλέει καὶ ἀγαθὰ ξυναπάσῃ Συρίῃ αἰτέει, οἱ δὲ τῶν εὐχωλέων ἀγχόθεν ἐπαΐουσιν. ἄλλοισιν δὲ δοκέει καὶ τάδε Δευκαλίωνος εἵνεκα ποιέεσθαι, ἐκείνης ξυμφορῆς μνήματα, ὁκότε οἱ ἄνθρωποι ἐς τὰ οὔρεα καὶ ἐς τὰ περιμήκεα τῶν δενδρέων ᾖσαν τὸ πολλὸν ὕδωρ ὀρρωδέοντες. ἐμοὶ μέν νυν καὶ τάδε ἀπίθανα. δοκέω γε μὲν Διονύσῳ σφέας καὶ τάδε ποιέειν, συμβάλλομαι δὲ τουτέοισι. φαλλοὺς ὅσοι Διονύσῳ ἐγείρουσι, ἐν τοῖσι φαλλοῖσι καὶ ἄνδρας ξυλίνους κατίζουσιν,

---

38. The exact position is now a matter of doubt (see the extracts in the Appendix (p. 94) and Hogarth in *Jour. Hell. Stud.*, xiv. p. 189). Pocock says: "About two hundred paces within the east gate there is raised ground, on which probably stood a temple of the Syrian goddess Atargatis. . . . I conjectured it to be about 200 feet in front. . . . I observed a low wall running from it to the gate . . . (*cf.* note 42, § 29). It is probable that all the space north of the temple belonged to it."

39. So the wall surrounding the royal Syro-Hittite city of Senjerli was doubled (Von Luschan and others, *Ausgr. in Sendschirli*, Berlin, 1893, etc.); likewise that of the Hittite township on Songrus Eyuk at Sakje Geuzi (*Liv. Annals of Arch.* v. 65). No traces of the original walls of Hierapolis remain: those described by our earliest travellers seem to be of Byzantine type. [See Appendix, pp. 95, 96, 99.]

40. The ὄργυια = 4 πήχεις, *i.e.*, 6 feet 1 inch. There is some general correspondence between the details supplied by Lucian and by Pocock. If the latter rightly judged the position we may infer that the temple was 600 feet in length, with a frontage of about 200 feet.

41. Above, § 16. Similarly twin pillars were erected in the temple of Hercules at Tyre (Herodotus, ii. 44), and in the temple of Solomon at Jerusalem (1 Kings, vii. 15, 21), "eighteen cubits high apiece right and left of the porch." At Paphos it

On the Syrian Goddess

28. The place whereon the temple is placed is a hill:[38] it lies nearly in the centre of the city, and is surrounded by a double wall.[39] Of the two walls the one is ancient; the other is not much older than our own times. The entrance to the temple faces the north; its size is about a hundred fathoms.[40] In this entrance those phalli stand which Dionysus erected:[41] they stand thirty fathoms high. Upon one of these a man mounts twice every year, and he abides on the summit of the phallus for the space of seven days. The reason of this ascent is given as follows: The people believe that the man who is aloft holds converse with the gods, and prays for good fortune for the whole of Syria, and that the gods from their neighbourhood hear his prayers. Others allege that this takes place in memory of the great calamity of Deukalion's time, when men climbed up to mountain tops and to the highest trees, in terror of the mass of waters. To me all this seems highly improbable, and I think that they observe this custom in honour of Dionysus, and I conjecture this from the following fact, that all those who rear phalli to Dionysus take care to place mannikins of wood on the phalli;

---

would appear from the coins that single pillars stood in the side chapels as well as the twin pillars and cone in the sanctuary. Gold models from Mykenæ show pairs of horns at the base and top of such pillars (Schuchhardt, *Schliemann's Excavations*, p. 199, fig. 183), suggesting emblems of generative power, and hence in this sense a phallic motive. On top of the horns is the dove, the emblem of the Goddess Mother. The question of original motive, however, is controversial. *Cf.* Evans, "Mykenæan Tree and Pillar Cult" (*Jour. Hell. Stud.*, 1907, pp. 99-203); Ramsay, "*Relig. of Asia Minor*," in Hastings' *Dict. Bible*, extra vol., p. 111; and the phallic character is disputed by Rob.-Smith, *Relig. Sem.*, p. 457. For the pillar cult in Asia Minor, see Ramsay, *loc. cit.* The pillar does not appear on Hittite mural decoration; but there is a remarkable monument at Fassiler, in Asia Minor, nearly 8 yards high, the width narrowing from 8 yards at the bottom to 1 yard at the top. Upon the base is carved a group showing a great figure upon two lions, with a smaller figure between the latter. The design has obvious Hittite characteristics, but the execution is crude (Ramsay, *Cities of St. Paul*, p. 134, fig. 7; *L. H.* pp. 175-176).

This class of emblem is to be distinguished from the sacred cones of the goddess in Syria and Asia Minor, such as are found at Mallus, Perga, Byblus, etc., *cf.* Fig. 6, p. 29.

42. *Cf.* § 28, where Lucian says that the entrance faced the north.

ὅτευ μὲν εἵνεκα ἐγὼ οὐκ ἐρέω. δοκέει δ' ὦν μοι, καὶ ὅδε ἐς ἐκείνου μίμησιν τοῦ ξυλίνου ἀνδρὸς ἀνέρχεται.

29. Ἡ δέ οἱ ἄνοδος τοιήδε: σειρῇ μικρῇ ἑωυτόν τε ἅμα καὶ τὸν φαλλὸν περιβάλλει, μετὰ δὲ ἐπιβαίνει ξύλων προσφυῶν τῷ φαλλῷ ὁκόσον ἐς χώρην ἄκρου ποδός: ἀνιὼν δὲ ἅμα ἀναβάλλει τὴν σειρὴν ἀμφοτέρωθεν ὅκωσπερ ἡνιοχέων. εἰ δέ τις τόδε μὲν οὐκ ὄπωπεν, ὄπωπεν δὲ φοινικοβατέοντας ἢ ἐν Ἀραβίῃ ἢ ἐν Αἰγύπτῳ ἢ ἄλλοθί κου, οἶδε τὸ λέγω.

Ἐπεὰν δὲ ἐς τέλος ἵκηται τῆς ὁδοῦ, σειρὴν ἑτέρην ἀφεὶς τὴν αὐτὸς ἔχει, μακρὴν ταύτην, ἀνέλκει τῶν οἱ θυμός, ξύλα καὶ εἵματα καὶ σκεύεα, ἀπὸ τῶν ἕδρην συνδέων ὁκοίην καλιὴν ἱζάνει, μίμνει τε χρόνον τῶν εἶπον ἡμερέων. πολλοὶ δὲ ἀπικνεόμενοι χρυσόν τε καὶ ἄργυρον, οἱ δὲ χαλκόν, τὰ νομίζουσιν, ἐς ἐχῖνον πρόσθε κείμενον κατιᾶσιν, λέγοντες τὰ οὐνόματα ἕκαστος. παρεστεὼς δὲ ἄλλος ἄνω ἀγγέλλει: ὁ δὲ δεξάμενος τοὔνομα εὐχωλὴν ἐς ἕκαστον ποιέεται, ἅμα δὲ εὐχόμενος κροτέει ποίημα χάλκεον, τὸ ἀείδει μέγα καὶ τρηχὺ κινεόμενον. εὕδει δὲ οὐδαμά: ἢν γάρ μιν ὕπνος ἕλῃ ποτέ, σκορπίος ἀνιὼν ἀνεγείρει τε καὶ ἀεικέα ἐργάζεται, καί οἱ ἥδε ἡ ζημίη τοῦ ὕπνου ἐπικέαται. τὰ μὲν ὦν ἐς τὸν σκορπίον μυθέονται ἱρά τε καὶ θεοπρεπέα: εἰ δὲ ἀτρεκέα ἐστίν, οὐκ ἔχω ἐρέειν. δοκέει δέ μοι, μέγα ἐς ἀγρυπνίην συμβάλλεται καὶ τῆς πτώσιος ἡ ὀρρωδίη. φαλλοβατέων μὲν δὴ πέρι τοσάδε ἀρκέει.

30. ὁ δὲ νηὸς ὁρέει μὲν ἐς ἠέλιον ἀνιόντα, εἶδος δὲ καὶ ἐργασίην ἐστὶν ὁκοίους νηοὺς ἐν Ἰωνίῃ ποιέουσιν. ἕδρη μεγάλη ἀνέχει ἐκ γῆς μέγαθος ὀργυιέων δυοῖν, ἐπὶ τῆς ὁ νηὸς ἐπικέαται. ἄνοδος ἐς αὐτὸν λίθου πεποίηται, οὐ κάρτα μακρή. ἀνελθόντι δὲ θαῦμα μὲν καὶ ὁ πρόνηος μέγα παρέχεται θύρῃσί τε ἤσκηται χρυσέῃσιν: ἔνδοθεν δὲ ὁ νηὸς χρυσοῦ τε πολλοῦ ἀπολάμπεται καὶ ἡ ὀροφὴ πᾶσα χρυσέη. ἀπόζει δὲ αὐτοῦ ὀδμὴ ἀμβροσίη ὁκοίη λέγεται τῆς χώρης τῆς Ἀραβίης,

---

43. See the design upon the remarkably instructive coin now at Vienna,

the reason of this I cannot say, but it seems to me that the ascent is made in imitation of the wooden mannikin.

29. To proceed, the ascent is made in this way; the man throws round himself and the phallus a small chain; afterwards he climbs up by means of pieces of wood attached to the phallus large enough to admit the end of his foot. As he mounts he jerks the chain up his own length, as a driver his reins. Those who have not seen this process, but who have seen those who have to climb palm trees in Arabia, or in Egypt, or any other place, will understand what I mean.

When he has climbed to the top, he lets down a different chain, a long one, and drags up anything that he wants, such as wood, clothing, and vases; he binds these together and sits upon them, as it were, on a nest, and he remains there for the space of time that I have mentioned. Many visitors bring him gold and silver, and some bring brass; then those who have brought these offerings leave them and depart, and each visitor gives his name. A bystander shouts the name up; and he on hearing the name utters a prayer for each donor; between the prayers he raises a sound on a brazen instrument which, on being shaken, gives forth a loud and grating noise. He never sleeps; for if at any time sleep surprises him, a scorpion creeps up and wakes him, and stings him severely; this is the penalty for wrongfully sleeping. This story about the scorpion is a sacred one, and one of the mysteries of religion; whether it is true I cannot say, but, as it seems to me, his wakefulness is in no small degree due to his fear of falling. So much then for the climbers of the phalli.

30. As for the temple, it looks to the rising sun.[42] In appearance, and in workmanship, it is like the temples which they build in Ionia, the foundation rises from the earth to the space of two fathoms, and on this rests the temple. The ascent to the temple is built of wood and not particularly wide; as you mount, even the great hall exhibits a wonderful spectacle and it is ornamented with golden doors. The temple within is ablaze with gold and the ceiling in its entirety is golden. There falls upon you also a divine fragrance such as is attributed to the region of Arabia,

καί σοι τηλόθεν ἀνιόντι προσβάλλει πνοιὴν κάρτα ἀγαθήν· καὶ ἢν αὖτις ἀπίῃς, οὐδαμὰ λείπεται, ἀλλά σευ τά τε εἵματα ἐς πολλὸν ἔχει τὴν πνοιὴν καὶ σὺ ἐς πάμπαν αὐτῆς μνήσεαι.

[31] Ἔνδοθεν δὲ ὁ νηὸς οὐκ ἁπλόος ἐστίν, ἀλλὰ ἐν αὐτῷ θάλαμος ἄλλος πεποίηται. ἄνοδος καὶ ἐς τοῦτον ὀλίγη· θύρῃσι δὲ οὐκ ἤσκηται, ἀλλὰ ἐς ἀντίον ἅπας ἀναπέπταται. ἐς μὲν ὦν τὸν μέγαν νηὸν πάντες ἐσέρχονται, ἐς δὲ τὸν θάλαμον οἱ ἱρέες μοῦνον, οὐ μέντοι πάντες οἱ ἱρέες, ἀλλὰ οἳ μάλιστα ἀγχίθεοί τέ εἰσιν καὶ οἷσι πᾶσα ἐς τὸ ἱρὸν μέλεται θεραπηίη. ἐν δὲ τῷδε εἵαται τὰ ἕδεα, ἥ τε Ἥρη καὶ τὸν αὐτοὶ Δία ἐόντα ἑτέρῳ οὐνόματι κληΐζουσιν. ἄμφω δὲ χρύσεοί τέ εἰσιν καὶ ἄμφω ἕζονται· ἀλλὰ τὴν μὲν Ἥρην λέοντες φέρουσιν, ὁ δὲ ταύροισιν ἐφέζεται.

[32] Καὶ δῆτα τὸ μὲν τοῦ Διὸς ἄγαλμα ἐς Δία πάντα ὁρῇ καὶ κεφαλὴν καὶ εἵματα καὶ ἕδρην, καί μιν οὐδὲ ἐθέλων ἄλλως εἰκάσεις. ἡ δὲ Ἥρη σκοπέοντί τοι πολυειδέα μορφὴν ἐκφανέει· καὶ τὰ μὲν ξύμπαντα ἀτρεκέϊ λόγῳ Ἥρη ἐστίν, ἔχει δέ τι καὶ Ἀθηναίης καὶ Ἀφροδίτης καὶ Σεληναίης καὶ Ῥέης καὶ Ἀρτέμιδος καὶ Νεμέσιος καὶ Μοιρέων. χειρὶ δὲ τῇ μὲν ἑτέρῃ σκῆπτρον ἔχει, τῇ ἑτέρῃ δὲ ἄτρακτον, καὶ ἐπὶ τῇ κεφαλῇ ἀκτῖνάς τε φορέει καὶ πύργον καὶ κεστὸν τῷ μούνην τὴν Οὐρανίην κοσμέουσιν. ἔκτοσθεν δέ οἱ χρυσός τε ἄλλος περικέαται καὶ λίθοι κάρτα πολυτελέες,

---

reproduced in Fig. 7. On the identification of "Hera," the lion goddess, and "Zeus," the bull-god, in the Hittite pantheon, see Introduction, pp. 8 ff., and Figs. 2, 3, 4. Macrobius speaks of them as "Hadad" and "Atargatis," names confirmed by inscriptions found at Delos (see p. 19). Lucian's description of the sanctuary, with its common shrine of "Hera" and "Zeus," and the details by which he distinguishes these deities, form the basis of our argument in the Introduction (pp. 9, 17, 20), that this god and goddess are identical with the chief Hittite male and female deities, who are "mated" in the sculptures at Yasily Kaya. The historical inference is that the origins of the temple date from the period of Hittite supremacy; and this conclusion is in seeming agreement with what Lucian says in § 17 of the antiquity of the original temple. Subsequently, as the Hittite power declined, their god lost predominance, and the cult of the Mother Goddess developed its local tendencies. The rites and institutions in the worship at Hierapolis which Lucian now proceeds to describe are naturally those

which breathes on you with a refreshing influence as you mount the long steps, and even when you have departed this fragrance clings to you; nay, your very raiment retains long that sweet odour, and it will ever remain in your memory.

31. But the temple within is not uniform. A special sacred shrine is reared within it; the ascent to this likewise is not steep, nor is it fitted with doors, but is entirely open as you approach it. The great temple is open to all; the sacred shrine to the priests alone and not to all even of these, but only to those who are deemed nearest to the gods and who have the charge of the entire administration of the sacred rites. In this shrine are placed the statues, one of which is Hera, the other Zeus, though they call him by another name. Both of these are golden, both are sitting; Hera is supported by lions, Zeus is sitting on bulls.

32. The effigy of Zeus recalls Zeus in all its details—his head, his robes, his throne; nor even if you wished it could you take him for another deity.[43] Hera, however, as you look at her will recall to you a variety of forms. Speaking generally she is undoubtedly Hera, but she has something of the attributes of Athene, and of Aphrodite, and of Selene, and of Rhea, and of Artemis, and of Nemesis, and of The Fates. In one of her hands she holds a sceptre, in the other a distaff; on her head she bears rays and a tower and she has a girdle wherewith they adorn none but Aphrodite of the sky.[44] And without she is gilt with gold, and gems of great price adorn her,

---

of his own time, but here and there (as in §§ 44, 47) traces of the original dual nature of the cult may be detected.

44. This description of the effigy distinguishes the original goddess from the naked or partly clad goddess, with hands to her breasts, with which she is commonly identified in later symbolism and modern interpretation. It accords, moreover, well with the pictures of the goddess upon coins, on which she is always fully clothed and usually girdled. (See Introduction, p. 11; also Frontispiece and Figs. 5, 7.) For a familiar aspect of Rhea (Kybele) see our illustration, Fig. 8, taken from a Roman lamp, published in Smith's *Small. Class. Dict.*—RHEA. A similar design appears on several lamps in the British Museum. For the girdle in Hittite art, see *L. H.*, p. 112 (Marash), p. 527 (Carchemish), etc.

τῶν οἱ μὲν λευκοί, οἱ δὲ ὑδατώδεες, πολλοὶ δὲ οἰνώδεες, πολλοὶ δὲ πυρώδεες, ἔτι δὲ ὄνυχες οἱ Σαρδῷοι πολλοὶ καὶ ὑάκινθοι καὶ σμάραγδοι, τὰ φέρουσιν Αἰγύπτιοι καὶ Ἰνδοὶ καὶ Αἰθίοπες καὶ Μῆδοι καὶ Ἀρμένιοι καὶ Βαβυλώνιοι. τὸ δὲ δὴ μέζονος λόγου ἄξιον, τοῦτο ἀπηγήσομαι· λίθον ἐπὶ τῇ κεφαλῇ φορέει· λυχνὶς καλέεται, οὔνομα δὲ οἱ τοῦ ἔργου ἡ συντυχίη. ἀπὸ τούτου ἐν νυκτὶ σέλας πολλὸν ἀπολάμπεται, ὑπὸ δέ οἱ καὶ ὁ νηὸς ἅπας οἷον ὑπὸ λύχνοισι φαείνεται. ἐν ἡμέρῃ δὲ τὸ μὲν φέγγος ἀσθενέει, ἰδέην δὲ ἔχει κάρτα πυρώδεα. καὶ ἄλλο θωυμαστόν ἐστιν ἐν τῷ ξοάνῳ. ἢν ἑστεὼς ἀντίος ἐσορέῃς, ἐς σὲ ὁρῇ καὶ μεταβαίνοντι τὸ βλέμμα ἀκολουθέει· καὶ ἢν ἄλλος ἑτέρωθεν ἱστορέῃ, ἴσα καὶ ἐς ἐκεῖνον ἐκτελέει.

33. Ἐν μέσῳ δὲ ἀμφοτέρων ἕστηκεν ξόανον ἄλλο χρύσεον, οὐδαμὰ τοῖσι ἄλλοισι ξοάνοισι εἴκελον. τὸ δὲ μορφὴν μὲν ἰδίην οὐκ ἔχει, φορέει δὲ τῶν ἄλλων θεῶν εἴδεα.

FIG. 7.—THE GOD AND GODDESS OF HIERAPOLIS
(From a Coin of the 3rd cent. A.D.)

some white, some sea-green, others wine-dark, others flashing like fire. Besides these there are many onyxes from Sardinia and the jacinth and emeralds, the offerings of the Egyptians and of the Indians, Ethiopians, Medes, Armenians, and Babylonians. But the greatest wonder of all I will proceed to tell: she bears a gem on her head called a Lychnis; it takes its name from its attribute. From this stone flashes a great light in the night-time, so that the whole temple gleams brightly as by the light of myriads of candles, but in the day-time the brightness grows faint; the gem has the likeness of a bright fire. There is also another marvel in this image: if you stand over against it, it looks you in the face, and as you pass it the gaze still follows you, and if another approaching from a different quarter looks at it, he is similarly affected.

33. Between the two there stands another image of gold, no part of it resembling the others. This possesses no special form of its own, but recalls the characteristics of other gods.

Fig. 8.—The Phrygian Goddess (Kybele) in the West
(From a Roman Lamp.)

καλέεται δὲ σημήιον καὶ ὑπ' αὐτῶν Ἀσσυρίων, οὐδέ τι οὔνομα ἴδιον αὐτῷ ἔθεντο, ἀλλ' οὐδὲ γενέσιος αὐτοῦ καὶ εἴδεος λέγουσιν. καί μιν οἱ μὲν ἐς Διόνυσον, ἄλλοι δὲ ἐς Δευκαλίωνα, οἱ δὲ ἐς Σεμίραμιν ἄγουσιν· καὶ γὰρ δὴ ὧν ἐπὶ τῇ κορυφῇ αὐτοῦ περιστερὴ χρυσέη ἐφέστηκεν, τοὔνεκα δὴ μυθέονται Σεμίραμιος ἔμμεναι τόδε σημήιον. ἀποδημέει δὲ δὶς ἑκάστου ἔτεος ἐς θάλασσαν ἐς κομιδὴν τοῦ εἶπον ὕδατος.

[34] Ἐν αὐτῷ δὲ τῷ νηῷ ἐσιόντων ἐν ἀριστερῇ κέαται πρῶτα μὲν θρόνος Ἡελίου, αὐτοῦ δὲ ἔδος οὐκ ἔνι· μούνου γὰρ Ἡελίου καὶ Σεληναίης ξόανα οὐ δεικνύουσιν. ὅτευ δὲ εἵνεκα ὧδε νομίζουσιν, ἐγὼ καὶ τόδε ἔμαθον. λέγουσι τοῖσι μὲν ἄλλοισι θεοῖσιν ὅσιον ἔμμεναι ξόανα ποιέεσθαι, οὐ γὰρ σφέων ἐμφανέα πάντεσι τὰ εἴδεα· Ἥλιος δὲ καὶ Σεληναίη πάμπαν ἐναργέες καὶ σφέας πάντες ὁρέουσι. κοίη ὦν αἰτίη ξοανουργίης τοῖσι ἐν τῷ ἠέρι φαινομένοισι;

[35] Μετὰ δὲ τὸν θρόνον τοῦτον κέαται ξόανον Ἀπόλλωνος, οὐκ οἷον ἐώθεε ποιέεσθαι· οἱ μὲν γὰρ ἄλλοι πάντες Ἀπόλλωνα νέον τε ἥγηνται καὶ πρωθήβην ποιέουσιν, μοῦνοι δὲ οὗτοι Ἀπόλλωνος γενειήτεω ξόανον δεικνύουσιν. καὶ τάδε ποιέοντες ἑωυτοὺς μὲν ἐπαινέουσιν, Ἑλλήνων δὲ κατηγορέουσιν καὶ ἄλλων ὁκόσοι Ἀπόλλωνα παῖδα θέμενοι ἱλάσκονται. αἰτίη δὲ ἥδε. δοκέει αὐτέοισι ἀσοφίη μεγάλη ἔμμεναι ἀτελέα ποιέεσθαι τοῖσι θεοῖσι τὰ εἴδεα, τὸ δὲ νέον ἀτελὲς ἔτι νομίζουσιν. ἐν δὲ καὶ ἄλλο τῷ σφετέρῳ Ἀπόλλωνι καινουργέουσι· μοῦνοι Ἀπόλλωνα εἵμασι κοσμέουσιν.

---

45. This object, "with characteristics of the other gods," etc., is hardly explained by the later structure of Roman character which appears upon the coin of the third century A.D. (*cf.* Fig.7, and p. 23); but in sculptures at Fraktin in Southern Asia Minor (*L. H.*, xlvii.) there are two groups. In the one there is a shrine and image of a god, whom a warrior-priest seems to be worshipping. In the other the Great Mother is enthroned, with a priestess pouring out an oblation before her. In each case between the deity and the worshipper there rises a special form of altar, with pedestal and flat round top (see Fig. 4, p. 17). The pedestal takes the form of a human body, from waist downwards, being swathed by many cross folds of a fringed cloth or garment. Upon the top is perched a dove or pigeon. The bird appears similarly placed on a similar altar at Yarre (Crowfoot, *Jour. Hell. Stud.* xix., 1899, fig. 4, pp. 40-45). The altar is shown

The Assyrians themselves speak of it as a symbol, but they have assigned to it no definite name. They have nothing to tell us about its origin, nor its form: some refer it to Dionysus; others to Deukalion; others to Semiramis; for its summit is crowned by a golden pigeon,⁴⁵ and this is why they allege that it is the effigy of Semiramis. It is taken down to the sea twice in every year to bring up the water of which I have spoken.⁴⁶

34. In the body of the temple, as you enter, there stands on the left hand side, a throne for the Sun god; but there is no image upon it, for the effigies of the Sun and Moon are not exhibited. I have learnt, however, the reasons of this practice. They say that religion does not forbid making effigies of the other deities, for the outward form of these deities is known to all; but the Sun and Moon are plain for all to see, and all men behold them. What boots it, therefore, to make effigies of those deities who offer themselves for all to gaze on?

35. Behind this throne stands an effigy of Apollo of an unusual character. All other sculptors think of Apollo as a youth, and represent him in the flower of his age. These artificers alone exhibit the Apollo of their statuary as bearded. They justify their action, and criticise the Greeks and others who set up Apollo as a boy, and appease him in that guise. Their reason is that it is a mark of ignorance to assign imperfect forms to the gods, and they look on youth as imperfection. They have also introduced another strange novelty in sculpture: they, and they alone, represent Apollo as robed.⁴

---

conventionally at Eyuk (see Fig. 3). For the dove in Hittite symbolism, see note 65, and Introduction, p. 11.

46. See above, § 13, and below, § 48.

47. It may reasonably be suspected that the empty throne for the sun-god (§ 34) was in reality an altar to this "bearded and robed Apollo." It is also clear that Lucian regards this form of the god as native; and it is of interest to consider what Oriental or Syrian deity is indicated, and for what reasons he became identified in the Greek mind with Apollo.

In the first place it is important to recall a passage from Macrobius, which amplifies Lucian's account and seems to confirm our surmise. In the *Saturnalia* (I. xvii. §§ 66, 67) he says: "The Hierapolitans, a Syrian people, assign all the powers and attributes of the sun to a bearded image which they call Apollo.

[36] ἔργων δὲ αὐτοῦ πέρι πολλὰ μὲν ἔχω εἰπεῖν, ἐρέω δὲ τὸ μάλιστα θωυμάζειν ἄξιον. πρῶτα δὲ τοῦ μαντηίου ἐπιμνήσομαι. μαντήια πολλὰ μὲν παρ' Ἕλλησι, πολλὰ δὲ καὶ παρ' Αἰγυπτίοισι, τὰ δὲ καὶ ἐν Λιβύῃ, καὶ ἐν τῇ δὲ Ἀσίῃ πολλά ἐστιν. ἀλλὰ τὰ μὲν οὔτε ἰρέων ἄνευ οὔτε προφητέων φθέγγονται, ὅδε δὲ αὐτός τε κινέεται καὶ τὴν μαντηίην ἐς τέλος αὐτουργέει. τρόπος δὲ αὐτῆς τοιόσδε. εὖτ' ἂν ἐθέλῃ χρησμηγορέειν, ἐν τῇ ἕδρῃ πρῶτα κινέεται, οἱ δέ μιν ἰρέες αὐτίκα ἀείρουσιν· ἢν δὲ μὴ ἀείρωσιν, ὁ δὲ ἰδρώει καὶ ἐς μέζον ἔτι κινέεται. εὖτ' ἂν δὲ ὑποδύντες φέρωσιν, ἄγει σφέας πάντῃ περιδινέων καὶ ἐς ἄλλον ἐξ ἑτέρου μεταπηδέων. τέλος ὁ ἀρχιερεὺς ἀντιάσας ἐπερέεταί μιν περὶ ἁπάντων πρηγμάτων· ὁ δὲ ἢν τι μὴ ἐθέλῃ ποιέεσθαι,

---

His face is represented with a long pointed beard, and he wears a *calathos* on his head. His body is protected with a breastplate. In his right hand he holds upright a spear, on the top of which is a small image of Victory; in his left is something like a flower. From the top of his shoulders there hangs down behind a cloak bordered with serpents. . . . Near him are eagles, represented as in flight: at his feet is the image of a woman, with two other female forms right and left; a dragon enfolds them with his coils." With the last sentence of this extract we are not concerned: it possibly refers to features of the shrine added since Lucian's days. We are left then with the conception of a native solar divinity, bearded and robed, and identified on general grounds with Apollo. Why, then, with Apollo?

The beard presents no difficulty, for in early art the Greek Apollo was frequently represented with this feature (*e.g.*, see Farnell, *Cults*, figs. xvii. and xxiii. and p. 329). In myth Apollo was twin-brother of Artemis; and in the *Iliad* he was definitely allied with the Trojans. Further, the attribute λύκιος or λύκειος suggests to some scholars an origin in Lycia; while others derive him from the East or from Egypt. However that may be, most scholars are agreed that some aspects of the god are associated with primitive Nature-worship, and there is a general suspicion of an Oriental or Asiatic element in his cult. (See especially the Oxford lectures of Wilamowitz, 1908, "Apollo," p. 30 ff.) This conclusion seems to be supported by the character and seasons of his festivals in Greece. In particular, the Theophania at Delphi, celebrating the return of the sun at springtime, and the πυανέψια at Athens, the harvest-thanksgiving, while natural to any pastoral country, are particularly apposite to the worship of the Great Mother. (For similar festivals in Hittite rites, *cf.* L. H., pp. 239, 359) Indeed, in § 49, Lucian describes a great festival of the springtime, at which noticeably goats, sheep and cattle were sacrificed; and horses are included in the list of sacred animals in § 41.

36. I have much to say about his works, and I will tell what is most worthy of admiration. First I will speak of the oracle. There are many oracles among the Greeks, and many, too, among the Egyptians, and again in Libya and in Asia there are many too. But these speak not, save by the mouth of priests and prophets: this one is moved by its own impulse, and carries out the divining process to the very end. The manner of his divination is the following: When he is desirous of uttering an oracle, he first stirs in his seat, and the priests straightway raise him up. Should they fail to raise him up, he sweats, and moves more violently than ever. When they approach him and bear him up,[48] he drives them round in a circle, and leaps on one after another. At last the high priest confronts him, and questions him on every subject. The god, if he disapproves of any action proposed,

---

There are, then, elements in the Cult of Apollo that had long been familiar to the nature-worshippers of Northern Syria and Asia Minor. The object suggesting a flower (*floris species*) in the hand of this god indicates, as Macrobius says, a god of vegetation; and possibly it replaced something more definitive, like ears of corn. The calathos we have seen already (note 33) to reflect the ancient conical hat of the Hittite age, and the spear is found in the hand of the warrior-god of Karabel, and in other examples of Hittite art (*L. H.*, pl. lxxv.). Now the local deity who most nearly combined these various attributes would be Sandan (or Sandes), who is figured on the Hittite sculpture of Ivriz (*L. H.*, pl. lvii.) as a god of agriculture, with corn and grapes; he is bearded and wears the Hittite dress and hat. There he was identified by the Greeks with Hercules. Professor Frazer has shown (*op. cit.*, pp. 110, 151 ff.) that Sandan bore to Baal much the same relation as the Hittite "Atys" to their "Zeus." But the youthful god, after the fall of the Hatti and their chief god, seems to have filled in the popular mind the place of the father god also, and to have become more and more identified with him (*cf.* Frazer, *op. cit.*, p. 236; *L. H.*, p. 360), like Atys with Zeus (Farnell, *Cults*, i., pp. 36, 37). In this way our Sandan-Atys might come to be regarded quite naturally as a sun-god (like Hadad-Zeus); and hence we should obtain a reasonable explanation for the identification of this deity with Apollo.

48. The image of the god is borne aloft on the shoulders of his priests in the Hittite sanctuary near Boghaz-Keui (*L. H.*, pl. lxv. and p. 239). Strabo (xii. iii. 32) relates a similar custom at Comana (Pontus) at the Exodi of the Goddess, also (xv. iii. 15) in the worship by the Persian settlers of Omanus at Zela in Cappadocia. So, too, the statue of Hadad in Assyria is shown borne by his priests on a representation from Nineveh (Layard, *Nineveh*, ii., 1849, pl. f. p. 451); and Macrobius (*Sat.* i. 17) tells us that the image of the analogous god of Heliopolis (*cf.* n. 26, p. 70) was carried about in a similar manner on a bier.

ὀπίσω ἀναχωρέει, ἢν δέ τι ἐπαινέῃ, ἄγει ἐς τὸ πρόσω τοὺς προφέροντας ὅκωσπερ ἡνιοχέων. οὕτως μὲν συναγείρουσι τὰ θέσφατα, καὶ οὔτε ἱρὸν πρῆγμα οὐδὲν οὔτε ἴδιον τούτου ἄνευ ποιέουσιν. λέγει δὲ καὶ τοῦ ἔτεος πέρι καὶ τῶν ὡρέων αὐτοῦ πασέων, καὶ ὁκότε οὐκ ἔρονται. λέγει δὲ καὶ τοῦ σημηίου πέρι, κότε χρή μιν ἀποδημέειν τὴν εἶπον ἀποδημίην.
37. ἐρέω δὲ καὶ ἄλλο, τὸ ἐμεῦ παρεόντος ἔπρηξεν. οἱ μέν μιν ἱρέες ἀείροντες ἔφερον, ὁ δὲ τοὺς μὲν ἐν γῇ κάτω ἔλιπεν, αὐτὸς δὲ ἐν τῷ ἠέρι μοῦνος ἐφορέετο.
38. Μετὰ δὲ τὸν Ἀπόλλωνα ξόανόν ἐστιν Ἄτλαντος, μετὰ δὲ Ἑρμέω καὶ Εἰλειθυίης.
39. τὰ μὲν ὦν ἐντὸς τοῦ νηοῦ ὧδε κεκοσμέαται· ἔξω δὲ βωμός τε κέαται μέγας χάλκεος, ἐν δὲ καὶ ἄλλα ξόανα μυρία χάλκεα βασιλέων τε καὶ ἱρέων· καταλέξω δὲ τῶν μάλιστα ἄξιον μνήσασθαι. ἐν ἀριστερῇ τοῦ νεὼ Σεμιράμιος ξόανον ἔστηκεν ἐν δεξιῇ τὸν νηὸν ἐπιδεικνύουσα. ἀνέστη δὲ δι᾽ αἰτίην τοιήνδε. ἀνθρώποισιν ὁκόσοι Συρίην οἰκέουσιν νόμον ἐποιέετο ἑαυτὴν μὲν ὅκως θεὸν ἱλάσκεσθαι, θεῶν δὲ τῶν ἄλλων καὶ αὐτῆς Ἥρης ἀλογέειν. καὶ ὧδε ἐποίεον. μετὰ δὲ ὥς οἱ θεόθεν ἀπίκοντο νοῦσοί τε καὶ συμφοραὶ καὶ ἄλγεα, μανίης μὲν ἐκείνης ἀπεπαύσατο καὶ θνητὴν ἑωυτὴν ὁμολόγεεν καὶ τοῖσιν ὑπηκόοισιν αὖτις ἐκέλευεν ἐς Ἥρην τρέπεσθαι. τοὔνεκα δὴ ἔτι τοιήδε ἀνέστηκεν, τοῖσιν ἀπικνεομένοισι τὴν Ἥρην ἱλάσκεσθαι δεικνύουσα, καὶ θεὸν οὐκέτι ἑωυτὴν ἀλλ᾽ ἐκείνην ὁμολογέουσα.

[40] εἶδον δὲ καὶ αὐτόθι Ἑλένης ἄγαλμα καὶ Ἑκάβης καὶ Ἀνδρομάχης καὶ Πάριδος καὶ Ἕκτορος καὶ Ἀχιλλέος. εἶδον δὲ καὶ Νειρέος εἶδος τοῦ Ἀγλαΐης, καὶ Φιλομήλην καὶ Πρόκνην ἔτι γυναῖκας, καὶ αὐτὸν Τηρέα ὄρνιθα, καὶ ἄλλο ἄγαλμα Σεμιράμιος, καὶ Κομβάβου τὸ κατέλεξα, καὶ Στρατονίκης κάρτα καλόν, καὶ Ἀλεξάνδρου αὐτῷ ἐκείνῳ εἴκελον, παρὰ δέ οἱ Σαρδανάπαλλος ἔστηκεν ἄλλῃ μορφῇ καὶ ἄλλῃ στολῇ.

---

49. Incidentally it is noteworthy that the group of emblems which distinguishes the king-priest at Boghaz-Keui (*L. H.*, pls. lxviii., lxxi.) is enclosed by columns which separate the celestial emblem, the winged disc, from the terrestrial, the boot. (*Cf.* Hom., *Odyssey*, i. 52.)

retreats into the background; if, however, he happens to approve it, he drives his bearers forward as if they were horses. It is thus that they gather the oracles, and they undertake nothing public or private without this preliminary. This god, too, speaks about the symbol, and points out when it is the due season for the expedition of which I spoke in connexion therewith.

37. I will speak of another wonder, too, which he performed in my presence. The priests were raising him aloft, but he left them on the ground, and was born aloft himself alone.

38. Behind Apollo is the statue of Atlas;[49] behind that, the statue of Hermes and Eilithyia.

39. Such, then, are the interior decorations of the temple; outside of it there stands a great altar of brass. It contains also countless other brazen effigies of kings and priests. I will mention those which seem most worthy of remembrance. To the left of the temple stands the image of Semiramis, pointing with her right hand to the temple. That image was erected to commemorate the following occurrence: The queen had issued a decree that all the Syrians should worship her as a deity, adding that they were to take no count of the others, not excepting even Hera; and they obeyed her decree. Afterwards, however, when disease and misfortune and grief were inflicted on her, she calmed down from her frenzied infatuation, and avowed herself a mere mortal, and ordered her subjects to turn again to Hera. This is why she stands to-day in this posture, pointing out Hera as the goddess whose grace is to be won, and confessing that she is not a goddess, but that Hera is indeed such.

40. I saw also the effigy of Helen, and of Hecuba, and of Andromache, and of Paris, and of Achilles. I saw also the statue of Nireus, the son of Aglaia, and of Philomela and Procne while yet women, and Tereus changed into a bird; and another effigy of Semiramis and one of Combabus and one of Stratonice of special beauty, and one of Alexander like to this. Sardanapalus stands by his side in a different form and in a different garb.

41. ἐν δὲ τῇ αὐλῇ ἄφετοι νέμονται βόες μεγάλοι καὶ ἵπποι καὶ ἀετοὶ καὶ ἄρκτοι καὶ λέοντες, καὶ ἀνθρώπους οὐδαμὰ σίνονται, ἀλλὰ πάντες ἱροί τέ εἰσι καὶ χειροήθεες. 42. ἱρέες δὲ αὐτοῖσι πολλοὶ ἀποδεδέχαται, τῶν οἱ μὲν τὰ ἱρήια σφάζουσιν, οἱ δὲ σπονδηφορέουσιν, ἄλλοι δὲ πυρφόροι καλέονται καὶ ἄλλοι παραβώμιοι. ἐπ' ἐμεῦ δὲ πλείονες καὶ τριηκοσίων ἐς τὴν θυσίην ἀπικνέοντο. ἐσθὴς δὲ αὐτέοισι πᾶσι λευκή, καὶ πῖλον ἐπὶ τῇ κεφαλῇ ἔχουσιν. ἀρχιερεὺς δὲ ἄλλος ἑκάστου ἔτεος ἐπιγίγνεται, πορφυρέην τε μοῦνος οὗτος φορέει καὶ τιάρῃ χρυσέῃ ἀναδέεται.

43. ἔστι δὲ καὶ ἄλλο πλῆθος ἀνθρώπων ἱρῶν αὐλητέων τε καὶ συριστέων καὶ Γάλλων, καὶ γυναῖκες ἐπιμανέες τε καὶ φρενοβλαβέες.

44. θυσίη δὲ δὶς ἑκάστης ἡμέρης ἐπιτελέεται, ἐς τὴν πάντες ἀπικνέονται. Διὶ μὲν ὦν κατ' ἡσυχίην θύουσιν οὔτε ἀείδοντες οὔτε αὐλέοντες· εὖτ' ἂν δὲ τῇ Ἥρῃ κατάρχωνται, ἀείδουσίν τε καὶ αὐλέουσιν καὶ κρόταλα ἐπικροτέουσιν. καί μοι τούτου πέρι σαφὲς οὐδὲν εἰπεῖν ἐδύναντο.

---

50. The ox and lion have been already noticed as sacred to the Hittite chief god and goddess, with whom they arc associated in religious art. (*Cf. L. H.*, pls. xliv., lxv.) The eagle appears (*a*) at Boghaz-Keui and at Eyuk as a double eagle identified with twin goddesses (*L. H.*, pl. lxv. and p. 269); and (*b*) in the gigantic carving near Yamoola (*L. H.*, pl. xlix.), where it is triumphing, it would seem, over lions. An inscription of Boghaz-Keui refers to a "house" or "temple of the eagle" (*Jour. R. A. S.*, 1909, p. 971). This bird would naturally seem to be an appropriate emblem of Zeus-Hadad, but there is nothing to substantiate this probability. The horse appears on Hittite sculptures only in an ordinary capacity; but in Anatolia in general developed sacred attributes. (*Cf.* Ramsay, "*Relig. of Asia Minor,*" in Hastings' *Dict. Bibl.*, extra vol., p. 115 b.)

51. The cap and "toga" of the priesthood on the Hittite sculptures distinguish them always from the deities and the people who are familiarly represented as wearing the tall conical hat, *e.g.*, the chief priests of Boghaz-Keui (*L. H.*, pls. lxviii., lxxi.), the king-priest at Eyuk (*ibid.*, pl. lxxii.), and at Sakje Geuzi, in Syria (pl. lxxxi.). On the election of the High Priest by the local worshippers compare

41. In the great court oxen of great size browsed horses, too, are there, and eagles and bears and lions, who never hurt mankind but are all sacred and all tame.[50]

42. Many priests also are in attendance, some of whom sacrifice the victims, others bring libations, others are called firebearers, and others altar attendants. In my presence more than 300 of these were present at a sacrifice; all had vestments of white and wore caps on their heads. Every year a new high priest is appointed.[51] He, and he alone, is clad in purple and crowned with a golden tiara.

43. Besides this there is another multitude of holy men, pipers, flute players,[52] and Galli; and women frenzied and fanatic.[53]

44. A sacrifice is offered up twice every day, and they are all present at this: To Zeus they sacrifice in silence, neither chanting nor playing, but when they sacrifice to Hera they sing, they pipe, and shake rattles. About this ceremony they could tell me nothing certain.[54]

---

the similar custom in vogue at the temple of Hadad and Atargatis at Delos (*Bull. Corr. Hell.*, 1882, p. 486).

52. *Cf.* the sculptures of Eyuk (*L. H.*, pl. lxxiii.), where three musicians are represented, with trumpet, bag-pipe and guitar. A lyre is figured in a sculpture from Marash (Humann and Puckstein, *Reisen*—Atlas, pl. xlvii. No. 2), and a guitar-player in the mural decorations of Senjerli (*Ausgrab.* III., pl. xxxviii.).

53. *Cf.* the accounts of Strabo concerning the temples at Comana of Cappadocia (bk. xii. ii. 3), where he states that it contained great multitudes of worshippers and temple servants, of the latter at the time he was there at least 6,000. So, too, at Venasa, in the "temple of Zeus" (Strabo, xii. ii. 6). *Cf.* the sculptures of Eyuk (*L. H.*, pl. lxxii.), where a number of priest-servants are represented in different avocations. On the rock-walls of the sanctuary near Boghaz-Keui numerous women as well as men are represented in the train of the male and female goddesses respectively; and in the small shrine of the youthful god which adjoins it there is a further group of men who, like those without, seem to be taking part in a ceremonial dance in rapid movement, with their sickles held aloft (*L. H.*, pl. lxix. and pp. 220, 227).

54. Notwithstanding the differences of ritual, the association of "Zeus" and "Hera" together in this paragraph is again significant of the original dual character of the cult.

45. ἔστι δὲ καὶ λίμνη αὐτόθι, οὐ πολλὸν ἑκὰς τοῦ ἱροῦ, ἐν τῇ ἰχθύες ἱροὶ τρέφονται πολλοὶ καὶ πολυειδέες. γίγνονται δὲ αὐτῶν ἔνιοι κάρτα μεγάλοι· οὗτοι δὲ καὶ οὐνόματα ἔχουσιν καὶ ἔρχονται καλεόμενοι· ἐπ᾽ ἐμέο δέ τις ἦν ἐν αὐτοῖσι χρυσοφορέων. ἐν τῇ πτέρυγι ποίημα χρύσεον αὐτέῳ ἀνακέατο, καί μιν ἐγὼ πολλάκις ἐθεησάμην, καὶ εἶχεν τὸ ποίημα.

46. βάθος δὲ τῆς λίμνης πολλόν. ἐγὼ μὲν οὐκ ἐπειρήθην, λέγουσι δ᾽ ὦν καὶ διηκοσίων ὀργυιέων πλέον ἔμμεναι. κατὰ μέσον δὲ αὐτῆς βωμὸς λίθου ἀνέστηκεν. δοκέοις ἂν ἄφνω πλώειν τέ μιν καὶ τῷ ὕδατι ἐποχέεσθαι, καὶ πολλοὶ ὧδε νομίζουσιν· ἐμοὶ δὲ δοκέει στῦλος ὑφεστεὼς μέγας ἀνέχειν τὸν βωμόν. ἔστεπται δὲ ἀεὶ καὶ θυώματα ἔχει, πολλοὶ δὲ καὶ ἑκάστης ἡμέρης κατ᾽ εὐχὴν ἐς αὐτὸν νηχόμενοι στεφανηφορέουσιν.

47. γίγνονται δὲ αὐτόθι καὶ πανηγύριές τε μέγισται, καλέονται δὲ ἐς τὴν λίμνην καταβάσιες, ὅτι ἐν αὐτῇσι ἐς τὴν λίμνην τὰ ἱρὰ πάντα κατέρχεται. ἐν τοῖσιν ἡ Ἥρη πρώτη ἀπικνέεται, τῶν ἰχθύων εἵνεκα, μὴ σφέας ὁ Ζεὺς πρῶτος ἴδηται· ἢν γὰρ τόδε γένηται, λέγουσιν ὅτι πάντες ἀπόλλυνται. καὶ δῆτα ὁ μὲν ἔρχεται ὀψόμενος, ἡ δὲ πρόσω ἱσταμένη ἀπείργει τέ μιν καὶ πολλὰ λιπαρέουσα ἀποπέμπει.

---

55. The sacred lake is still conspicuous. *Cf.* Maundrell, *op. cit.* p. 154: "On the west side is a deep pit, of about 100 yards diameter; it . . . seemed to have had great buildings all round it, with the pillars and ruins of which it is now almost filled up, . . . but . . . there was still water in it." Chesney, *Exped. Euphrat.* i. 516: "a rocky hollow." Hogarth (*Jour. Hell. Stud.* xiv. p. 187) describes also "the scanty remains of a stepped quay wall or revetment, with water stairs at intervals."

The Hittite river-gods are invoked in witness of their treaty with Egypt (c. 1271 B.C.). *Cf.* also Ramsay, *Luke the Physician*, pp. 171 *et seq.*; *Pauline and other Studies*, pp. 172, 173. On the general question of sacred waters in Syria, see Robertson-Smith, *op. cit.* pp. 170-172; Frazer, *op. cit.* pp. 22-23.

56. See also § 14, n. 28. No local tradition of this seems to survive, but Xenophon (*Anabasis*, I. iv. 9) records a parallel case of "tame fish looked upon as gods" in the Chalus, near Aleppo. Modern instances near Doliche, just north

45. There is too a lake[55] in the same place, not far from the temple in which many sacred fishes of different kinds are reared[56] Some of these grow to a great size; they are called by names, and approach when called. I saw one of these ornamented with gold, and on its back fin a golden design was dedicated to the temple. I have often seen this fish, and he certainly carried this design.

46. The depth of the lake is immense. I never tested it myself, but they say that it is in depth more than 200 fathoms. In the midst of this lake stands an altar of stone. You would think at first sight that it was floating and moving in the water, and many deem that it is so. The truth seems to me that it is supported by a column of great size, based on the bottom of the lake. It is always decked with ribbons, and spices are therein, and many every day swim in the lake with crowns on their heads performing their acts of adoration.

47. At this lake great assemblies meet, and these are called descents into the lake because all their deities go down into this lake, amongst whom Hera[57] first advances so that Zeus may not see the fish first, for if this were to happen they say that one and all would perish. And Zeus comes indeed intending to see these fish, but she, standing before him, keeps hint at bay, and with many supplications holds him off.

---

of Aintab, and elsewhere in Syria, are described by Cumont (*Oriental Relig.*, p. 245, note 36) and Hogarth (*op. cit.*, p. 188). So also near the mosque of Edessa (Sachau, *Reise*, p. 196); and in Asia Minor, at Tavshanli, on the Rhyndacus, sacred fish are still preserved in a large cistern (Cumont, *loc. cit.*, ap. Munro).

Atargatis, according to the form of the legend given by the scholiast on Germanicus' "Aratus" was born of an egg which the sacred fishes found in the Euphrates and pushed ashore. On the general subject, see Robertson-Smith, *op. cit.* p. 292, also pp. 174-175 and 219.

57. *Cf.* the legend that Hera bathed in the Chaboras, a Mesopotamian tributary of the Euphrates, after her marriage with Zeus (Ælian, *Nat. Animalium*, xii. 30). The further reference to fishes implies their sanctity to the goddess, and to this extent reveals Atargatis as a fish-goddess (see note 25). This is, however, clearly not her chief character at Hierapolis.

48. μέγισται δὲ αὐτοῖσι πανηγύριες αἳ ἐς θάλασσαν νομίζονται. ἀλλ' ἐγὼ τούτων πέρι σαφὲς οὐδὲν ἔχω εἰπεῖν· οὐ γὰρ ἦλθον αὐτὸς οὐδὲ ἐπειρήθην ταύτης τῆς ὁδοιπορίης. τὰ δὲ ἐλθόντες ποιέουσιν, εἶδον καὶ ἀπηγήσομαι. ἀγγήιον ἕκαστος ὕδατι σεσαγμένον φέρουσιν, κηρῷ δὲ τάδε σεσήμανται. καί μιν οὐκ αὐτοὶ λυσάμενοι χέονται, ἀλλ' ἔστιν ἀλεκτρυὼν ἱρός, οἰκέει δὲ ἐπὶ τῇ λίμνῃ, ὃς ἐπεὶ σφέων δέξηται τὰ ἀγγήια, τήν τε σφρηγῖδα ὁρῇ καὶ μισθὸν ἀρνύμενος ἀνά τε λύει τὸν δεσμὸν καὶ τὸν κηρὸν ἀπαιρέεται· καὶ πολλαὶ μνέες ἐκ τουτέου τοῦ ἔργου τῷ ἀλεκτρυόνι ἀγείρονται. ἔνθεν δὲ ἐς τὸν νηὸν αὐτοὶ ἐνείκαντες σπένδουσί τε καὶ θύσαντες ὀπίσω ἀπονοστέουσιν.

49. ὁρτέων δὲ πασέων τῶν οἶδα μεγίστην τοῦ εἴαρος ἀρχομένου ἐπιτελέουσιν, καί μιν οἱ μὲν πυρήν, οἱ δὲ λαμπάδα καλέουσιν. θυσίην δὲ ἐν αὐτῇ τοιήνδε ποιέουσιν. δένδρεα μεγάλα ἐκκόψαντες τῇ αὐλῇ ἑστᾶσι, μετὰ δὲ ἀγινέοντες αἶγάς τε καὶ ὄϊας καὶ ἄλλα κτήνεα ζωὰ ἐκ τῶν δενδρέων ἀπαρτέουσιν· ἐν δὲ καὶ ὄρνιθες καὶ εἵματα καὶ χρύσεα καὶ ἀργύρεα ποιήματα. ἐπεὰν δὲ ἐντελέα πάντα ποιήσωνται, περιενείκαντες τὰ ἱρὰ περὶ τὰ δένδρεα πυρὴν ἐνιᾶσιν, τὰ δὲ αὐτίκα πάντα καίονται. ἐς ταύτην τὴν ὁρτὴν πολλοὶ ἄνθρωποι ἀπικνέονται ἔκ τε Συρίης καὶ τῶν πέριξ χωρέων πασέων, φέρουσίν τε τὰ ἑωυτῶν ἱρὰ ἕκαστοι καὶ τὰ σημήια ἕκαστοι ἔχουσιν ἐς τάδε μεμιμημένα.

---

58. On the local use of the word "sea," meaning thereby the Euphrates, see note 23. On the further subject of the narrative, *cf.* §§ 13, 36. It is of interest to notice that Pliny (*Nat. Hist.* xxxi. 37) describes a method of filtering sea water into empty sealed vessels.

59. Ἀλεκτρυὼν ἱρός. The narrative is unintelligible unless we suppose that the words by allusion or textual change signify some special priestly office. Thus Blunt (*Works of Lucian*, London: Briscoe, 1711, p. 267) translates "a sacred cock, or priest, called Alectryo." Is it possible that the word in this sense was in common vogue, on the analogy of the Latin *Gallus*, a cock? (*Cf.* an inscription on an urn in the Lateran Museum at Rome, cited by Frazer, *op. cit.* p. 233, on which the cock is used as emblem of the Attis-priest, with a punning reference to the word.) Belin de Ballu, in his translation (Paris, 1789), v. 178, following Paulmier de Grentruéuil, unhesitatingly substitutes Γάλλος, and translates accordingly.

48. But the greatest of these sacred assemblies are those held on the sea coast.[58] About these, however, I have nothing certain to say. I was never present at their celebrations, nor did I undertake the journey thither; but I did see what they do on their return, and I will at once tell you. Each member of the assembly carries a vessel full of water. The vessels are sealed with wax; those who carry the water do not unseal the vessels and then pour out the water; but there is a certain holy cock[59] who dwells hard by the lake. This bird, on receiving the vessels from the bearers, inspects the seal, and after receiving a reward for this action he breaks the thread and picks away the wax, and many minae are collected by the cock by this operation. After this the bearers carry the water into the temple and pour it forth, and they depart when the sacrifice is finished.

49. The greatest of the festivals that they celebrate is that held in the opening of spring; some call this the Pyre, others the Lamp. On this occasion the sacrifice is performed in this way. They cut down tall trees and set them up in the court; then they bring goats and sheep and cattle and hang them living to the trees; they add to these birds and garments and gold and silver work. After all is finished, they carry the gods around the trees and set fire under;[60] in a moment all is in a blaze. To this solemn rite a great multitude flocks from Syria and all the regions around. Each brings his own god and the statues which each has of his own gods.

---

60. In this festival of the Pyre at Heliopolis one or two details may profitably be noticed. The "tall trees" suggest the pine, sacred to Attis. (*Cf.*, *inter alia*, Farnell, Cults, p. 645, and Frazer, *op. cit.*, p. 222.) It is possible that in the sculptures of Boghaz-Keui the objects on which the high priest stands (*L. H.*, pl. lxviii.) are indeed fir-cones. Goats and sheep we have seen led to sacrifice at Eyuk; the former animal is frequently represented in association with the Hittite chief god, and was no doubt sacred to him. "Cattle" indicate the bull, the emblem of the great god, and the cow with which his consort might be reciprocally identified. *Cf.* Pausanias (XI., iii. 7), where the bull and cow are seen to be sacred to Zeus and Hera respectively; and compare especially the details of the Dædala with this holocaust. The hanging of garments or shreds of them on trees near sacred places, or trees themselves, is a common practice in the East and in Egypt to-day. (*Cf.* also Rob.-Smith, *op. cit.*, p. 335.) In the last words of the paragraph it is significant that no special mention is made of a goddess in connection with this rite.

50. ἐν ῥητῇσι δὲ ἡμέρῃσι τὸ μὲν πλῆθος ἐς τὸ ἱρὸν ἀγείρονται, Γάλλοι δὲ πολλοὶ καὶ τοὺς ἔλεξα, οἱ ἱροὶ ἄνθρωποι, τελέουσι τὰ ὄργια, τάμνονταί τε τοὺς πήχεας καὶ τοῖσι νώτοισι πρὸς ἀλλήλους τύπτονται. πολλοὶ δὲ σφίσι παρεστεῶτες ἐπαυλέουσι, πολλοὶ δὲ τύμπανα παταγέουσιν, ἄλλοι δὲ ἀείδουσιν ἔνθεα καὶ ἱρὰ ᾄσματα. τὸ δὲ ἔργον ἐκτὸς τοῦ νηοῦ τόδε γίγνεται, οὐδὲ ἐσέρχονται ἐς τὸν νηὸν ὁκόσοι τόδε ποιέουσιν.

51. ἐν ταύτῃσι τῇσι ἡμέρῃσι καὶ Γάλλοι γίγνονται. ἐπεὰν γὰρ οἱ ἄλλοι αὐλέωσί τε καὶ ὄργια ποιέωνται, ἐς πολλοὺς ἤδη ἡ μανίη ἀπικνέεται, καὶ πολλοὶ ἐς θέην ἀπικόμενοι μετὰ δὲ τοιάδε ἔπρηξαν. καταλέξω δὲ καὶ τὰ ποιέουσιν. ὁ νεηνίης ὅτῳ τάδε ἀποκέαται ῥίψας τὰ εἵματα μεγάλῃ βοῇ ἐς μέσον ἔρχεται καὶ ξίφος ἀναιρέεται· τὸ δὲ πολλὰ ἔτη, ἐμοὶ δοκέει, καὶ τοῦτο ἕστηκε. λαβὼν δὲ αὐτίκα τάμνει ἑωυτὸν θέει τε διὰ τῆς πόλιος καὶ τῇσι χερσὶ φέρει τὰ ἔταμεν. ἐς ὁκοίην δὲ οἰκίην τάδε ἀπορρίψει, ἐκ ταύτης ἐσθῆτά τε θηλέην καὶ κόσμον τὸν γυναικήιον λαμβάνει. τάδε μὲν ἐν τῇσι τομῇσι ποιέουσιν.

52. ἀποθανόντες δὲ Γάλλοι οὐκ ὁμοίην ταφὴν τοῖσιν ἄλλοισι θάπτονται, ἀλλ' ἐὰν ἀποθάνῃ Γάλλος, ἑταῖροί μιν ἀείραντες ἐς τὰ προάστεια φέρουσιν, θέμενοι δὲ αὐτὸν καὶ τὸ φέρτρον τῷ ἐκόμισαν, ὕπερθε λίθοις βάλλουσιν, καὶ τάδε πρήξαντες ὀπίσω ἀπονοστέουσιν. φυλάξαντες δὲ ἑπτὰ ἡμερέων ἀριθμὸν οὕτως ἐς τὸ ἱρὸν ἐσέρχονται· πρὸ δὲ τουτέων ἢν ἐσέλθωσιν, οὐκ ὅσια ποιέουσιν.

53. νόμοισι δὲ ἐς ταῦτα χρέωνται τουτέοισι. ἢν μέν τις αὐτέων νέκυν ἴδηται, ἐκείνην τὴν ἡμέρην ἐς τὸ ἱρὸν οὐκ ἀπικνέεται, τῇ ἑτέρῃ δὲ καθήρας ἑωυτὸν ἐσέρχεται. αὐτῶν δὲ τῶν οἰκείων τοῦ νέκυος ἕκαστοι φυλάξαντες ἀριθμὸν ἡμερέων τριήκοντα καὶ τὰς κεφαλὰς ξυράμενοι ἐσέρχονται· πρὶν δὲ τάδε ποιῆσαι, οὔ σφίσι ἐσιέναι ὅσιον.

---

61. *Cf.* the rites surviving in the worship of Kybele and Attis in Rome. For a description and bibliog., see Cumont, *op. cit.*, ch. iii., Asia Minor, p. 46 *ff*., and Frazer, *op. cit.*, p. 233.

50. On certain days a multitude flocks into the temple, and the Galli in great numbers, sacred as they are, perform the ceremonies of the men and gash their arms and turn their backs to be lashed. [61] Many bystanders play on the pipes the while many beat drums; others sing divine and sacred songs. All this performance takes place outside the temple, and those engaged in the ceremony enter not into the temple.

51. During these days they are made Galli. As the Galli sing and celebrate their orgies, frenzy falls on many of them and many who had come as mere spectators afterwards are found to have committed the great act. I will narrate what they do. Any young man who has resolved on this action, strips off his clothes, and with a loud shout bursts into the midst of the crowd, and picks up a sword from a number of swords which I suppose have been kept ready for many years for this purpose. He takes it and castrates himself [62] and then runs wild through the city, bearing in his hands what he has cut off. He casts it into any house at will, and from this house he receives women's raiment and ornaments. [63] Thus they act during their ceremonies of castration.

52. The Galli, when dead, are not buried like other men, but when a Gallus dies his companions carry him out into the suburbs, and laying him out on the bier on which they had carried him they cover him with stones, and after this return home. They wait then for seven days, after which they enter the temple. Should they enter before this they would be guilty of blasphemy.

53. The laws which they observe are the following: Anyone who has seen a corpse may not enter the temple the same day; but afterwards, when he has purified himself, he enters. But those who are of the family of the corpse wait for thirty days, and after shaving their heads they enter the temple, but before they have done this it is forbidden.

---

62. On this custom, which is specially characteristic of the worship of the goddess, see, *inter alia*, Frazer, *op. cit.*, p. 224; Farnell, *Greece and Babylon*, pp. 256, 257; also our Introduction, p. 3, n. 10

63. *Cf.* § 15, above, n. 7. On the general aspect of this custom, see, especially, Frazer, *op. cit.*, Appendix iv. p. 428.

54. θύουσιν δὲ βόας ἄρσενάς τε καὶ θήλεας καὶ αἶγας καὶ ὄϊας. σύας δὲ μοῦνον ἐναγέας νομίζοντες οὔτε θύουσιν οὔτε σιτέονται. ἄλλοι δ' οὐ σφέας ἐναγέας, ἀλλὰ ἱροὺς νομίζουσιν. ὀρνίθων τε αὐτέοισι περιστερὴ δοκέει χρῆμα ἱρότατον καὶ οὐδὲ ψαύειν αὐτέων δικαιέουσιν· καὶ ἢν ἀέκοντες ἅψωνται, ἐναγέες ἐκείνην τὴν ἡμέρην εἰσί. τοὔνεκα δὲ αὐτέοισι σύννομοί τέ εἰσι καὶ ἐς τὰ οἰκεῖα ἐσέρχονται καὶ τὰ πολλὰ ἐν γῇ νέμονται.
55. λέξω δὲ καὶ τῶν πανηγυριστέων τὰ ἕκαστοι ποιέουσιν.

ἀνὴρ εὖτ' ἂν ἐς τὴν ἱρὴν πόλιν πρῶτον [ἀπέρχηται], κεφαλὴν μὲν ὅδε καὶ ὀφρύας ἐξύρατο, μετὰ δὲ ἱρεύσας ὄϊν τὰ μὲν ἄλλα κρεουργέει τε καὶ εὐωχέεται, τὸ δὲ νάκος χαμαὶ θέμενος ἐπὶ τούτου ἐς γόνυ ἕζεται, πόδας δὲ καὶ κεφαλὴν τοῦ κτήνεος ἐπὶ τὴν ἑωυτοῦ κεφαλὴν ἀναλαμβάνει· ἅμα δὲ εὐχόμενος αἰτέει τὴν μὲν παρεοῦσαν θυσίην δέκεσθαι, μέζω δὲ ἐσαῦτις ὑπισχνέεται. τελέσας δὲ ταῦτα, τὴν κεφαλὴν αὐτοῦ τε στέφεται καὶ τῶν ἄλλων ὁκόσοι τὴν αὐτὴν ὁδὸν ἀπικνέονται,

---

64. No actual act of sacrifice is represented in Hittite art, though at Eyuk and Malâtia goats and rams are seen led to the altar of the god. The general subject of burnt sacrifice and holocausts among the Semites is discussed fully by Rob.-Smith, *op. cit.*, x. xi., and numerous special rites of extreme interest are described by Frazer, *op. cit.* On the sacred animals of Asia Minor, see also Ramsay, *Relig. of Asia Minor, op. cit.*, pp. 114, etc.

65. On the sanctity and abhorrence of the pig, see especially, Ramsay, *op. cit.* p. 115 b, and *Hist. Geog. of Asia Minor*, p. 32, where he points out that the Halys River divided these two points of view. See also Robertson-Smith, *op. cit.* pp. 153, 392, n., 448; and the discussion of his theory of Adonis as a swine-god by Farnell, *Cults*, p. 645. For the swine in connection with the Cult of Set in Egypt, *cf.* Newberry, in *Klio*, xii. (1912), p. 397 ff.

66. *Cf.* also § 16. This statement is confirmed by Xenophon, Anabasis, I. iv. 9. According to Ælian (Nat. Ann. iv. 2), the dove was an especially sacred companion to Astarte, and this is borne out by archaic clay figurines of the goddess from Phœnicia, Asia Minor, Rhodes, Delos, Athens and Etruria. These are ascribed to "Aphrodite" by Fürtwangler (Roscher's *Lexikon f. Griech. u. Röm. Mythologie*, p. 410, *q.v.*); but are indistinguishable as to character and provenance from the original deity. (*Cf.* also Ed. Meyer, in the same, art. Astarte.) In Babylonian and Assyrian art and mythology the bird does not seem to appear in the same inseparable association with Ishtar, though we have the suggestive passage: "Like a lonely dove, I rest" (Pinches, *op. cit.*, col. iii. ll. 1, 2). On this

54. They sacrifice bulls and cows alike and goats and sheep;[64] pigs alone, which they abominate, are neither sacrificed nor eaten. Others look on swine without disgust, but as holy animals.[65] Of birds the dove seems the most holy to them,[66] nor do they think it right to harm these birds, and if anyone have harmed them unknowingly they are unholy for that day, and so when the pigeons dwell with the men they enter their rooms and commonly feed on the ground.

55. I will speak, too, about those who come to these sacred meetings and of what they do. As soon as a man comes to Hierapolis he shaves his head and his eyebrows;[67] afterwards he sacrifices a sheep[68] and cuts up its flesh and eats it; he then lays the fleece on the ground, places his knee on it, but puts the feet and head of the animal on his own head and at the same time he prays that the gods may vouchsafe to receive him, and he promises a greater victim hereafter. When this is performed he crowns his head with a garland and the heads of all those engaged in the same procession.

---

point Mr. L. W. King writes: "In the earlier periods there is no evidence that a bird was associated with Ishtar, and I have little doubt that the association was a comparatively late addition to her cult. Of course the myth of the Allatu bird is early, but can hardly be connected with the symbolic or votive bird under her Phœnician form" (Letter dated Sept. 7, 1912). Diodorus relates how the child Semiramis was fed by doves, and how eventually she took flight to heaven in the appearance of this bird.

In Hittite art of Asia Minor, however, the bird appears in association with the enshrined Goddess-mother, at Yarre (*Jour. Hell. Stud.* xix. fig. 4), at Fraktin (Fig. 7), and in two carvings from Marash (*L. H.*, pp. 119, 151, 164).

In glyptic art the evidence of association is confirmatory (see Hayes Ward, *Seal Cylinders of Western Asia*, pp. 293, etc., especially Nos. 898, 904, 908, 943). With the naked goddess, who may be of Syrian origins (*ibid.* p. 162), and is found represented on a sculpture of Carchemish (*L. H.*, p. 128), but not elsewhere on Hittite monuments, the bird appears only sporadically.

Among the Semites the pigeon was peculiarly sacred (Robertson-Smith, *op. cit.* p. 294), and sacrificed only on special occasions (*ibid.* p. 219; *cf.* also Leviticus xix. 4, 49 Numbers, vi. 10). The sacred character of the bird does not seem to survive in any form.

67. *Cf.* § 60.

68. *Cf.* especially Rob.-Smith, *op. cit.* p. 477 *ff.*

ἄρας δὲ ἀπὸ τῆς ἑωυτοῦ ὁδοιπορέει, ὕδασί τε ψυχροῖσι χρεόμενος λουτρῶν τε καὶ πόσιος εἵνεκα καὶ ἐς πάμπαν χαμοκοιτέων: οὐ γάρ οἱ εὐνῆς ἐπιβῆναι ὅσιον πρὶν τήν τε ὁδὸν ἐκτελέσαι καὶ ἐς τὴν ἑωυτοῦ αὖτις ἀπικέσθαι.

56. ἐν δὲ τῇ ἱρῇ πόλει ἐκδέκεταί μιν ἀνὴρ ξεινοδόκος ἀγνοέοντα: ῥητοὶ γὰρ δὴ ὧν ἑκάστης πόλιος αὐτόθι ξεινοδόκοι εἰσίν, καὶ τόδε πατρόθεν οἴκοι δέκονται. καλέονται δὲ ὑπὸ Ἀσσυρίων οἵδε διδάσκαλοι, ὅτι σφίσι πάντα ὑπηγέονται.

57. θύουσι δὲ οὐκ ἐν αὐτῷ τῷ ἱρῷ, ἀλλ' ἐπεὰν παραστήσῃ τῷ βωμῷ τὸ ἱρήιον, ἐπισπείσας αὖτις ἄγει ζῳὸν ἐς τὰ οἰκεῖα, ἐλθὼν δὲ κατ' ἑωυτὸν θύει τε καὶ εὔχεται.

58. ἔστιν δὲ καὶ ἄλλης θυσίης τρόπος τοιόσδε. στέψαντες τὰ ἱρήια, ζῳὰ ἐκ τῶν προπυλαίων ἀπιᾶσιν, τὰ δὲ κατενεχθέντα θνήσκουσιν. ἔνιοι δὲ καὶ παῖδας ἑωυτῶν ἐντεῦθεν ἀπιᾶσιν, οὐκ ὁμοίως τοῖς κτήνεσιν, ἀλλ' ἐς πήρην ἐνθέμενοι χειρὶ κατάγουσιν, ἅμα δὲ αὐτέοισιν ἐπικερτομέοντες λέγουσιν ὅτι οὐ παῖδες, ἀλλὰ βόες εἰσίν.

59. στίζονται δὲ πάντες, οἱ μὲν ἐς καρπούς, οἱ δὲ ἐς αὐχένας: καὶ ἀπὸ τοῦδε ἅπαντες Ἀσσύριοι στιγματηφορέουσιν.

60. ποιέουσι δὲ καὶ ἄλλο μούνοισι Ἑλλήνων Τροιζηνίοισι ὁμολογέοντες. λέξω δὲ καὶ τὰ ἐκεῖνοι ποιέουσιν. Τροιζήνιοι τῇσι παρθένοισι καὶ τοῖσιν ἠιθέοισι νόμον ἐποιήσαντο μή μιν ἄλλως γάμον ἰέναι, πρὶν Ἱππολύτῳ κόμας κείρασθαι: καὶ ὧδε ποιέουσιν. τοῦτο καὶ ἐν τῇ ἱρῇ πόλει γίγνεται.

---

69. The libation is a feature of Hittite worship represented on several sculptures, *e.g.*, at Fraktin and at Malâtia (see Fig. 1, p. 4). At the latter place live animals (rams) are shown in the sculpture (*L. H.*, pl. xliv.) behind the priest, being led by an attendant. This is not shown in our illustration, in which also the Hittite hieroglyphics are omitted from the field for the sake of clearness. These sculptures have been lately removed, it is reported, to Constantinople.

70. The special character of this sacrifice is strongly suggestive of a totemistic influence. On the general aspect of human sacrifice among the Semites, *cf.* Rob.-Smith, *op. cit.*, pp. 371, 464. On human sacrifice in the Cult of Dionysus, *cf.* Frazer, *op. cit.*, p. 332. Children were sacrificed to Moloch, who was identified with Cronos, an original deity of vegetation (*cf.* Farnell, Culls, p. 28, n.). Attempts have been made (*cf.* Dussaud, *Rev. Arch.*, *loc. cit.*, ap. Movers; Six,

Starting from his house he passes into the road, previously bathing himself and drinking cold water. He always sleeps on the ground, for he may not enter his bed till the completion of his journey.

56. In the city of Hierapolis a public host receives him, suspecting nothing, for there are special hosts attached to each city, and these receive each guest according to his country. These are called by the Assyrians teachers, because they teach them all the solemn rites.

57. They sacrifice victims not in the temple itself, but when the sacrificer has placed his victim at the altar and poured a libation[69] he brings the animal home alive, and returning to his own house he slays his victim and utters prayers.

58. There is also another method of sacrifice, as follows: They adorn live victims with ribbons and throw them headlong down from the temple's entrance, and these naturally die after their fall. Some actually throw their own children down, not as they do the cattle, but they sew them into a sack and toss them down, visiting them with curses and declaring that they are not their children, but are cows.[70]

59. They all tattoo themselves—some on the hands and some on the neck—and so it comes that all the Assyrians bear stigmata.[71]

60. They have another curious custom, in which they agree with the Trœzenians alone of the Greeks. I will explain this too. The Trœzenians have made a law for their maidens and youths alike never to marry till they have dedicated their locks to Hippolytus; and this they do. It is the same at Hierapolis.

Rev. Num., *loc. cit.*) to identify the god of Hierapolis with Cronos. While we cannot accept the theory, this field of enquiry is attractive; and the suggested identity might arise in myth by grouping the god as father of the goddess's son in a natural triad.

71. *Cf.* Pliny, *Nat. Hist.*, vi. 4, and xxii. 2. On this subject, *cf.* Rob.-Smith, *op. cit.*, p. 334, note 1. In the Sudan, according to Bruce, some of the tribes tattooed their stomachs, sides and backs, as with fish-scales. Professor Strong reminds us that there have been found a number of bodies of Nubians of the time of the Middle Empire (*c.* 2000 B.C.) with definite tattooing; and the patterns pricked upon the skin of these desiccated bodies were identical with those painted on the dolls buried with them. *Cf.* Dr. Elliot Smith, *The Ancient Egyptians*, p. 56.

οἱ μὲν νεηνίαι τῶν γενείων ἀπάρχονται, τοῖς δὲ νέοισι πλοκάμους ἱροὺς ἐκ γενετῆς ἀπιᾶσιν, τοὺς ἐπεὰν ἐν τῷ ἱρῷ γένωνται, τάμνουσίν τε καὶ ἐς ἄγγεα καταθέντες οἱ μὲν ἀργύρεα, πολλοὶ δὲ χρύσεα ἐν τῷ νηῷ προσηλώσαντες ἀπίασιν ἐπιγράψαντες ἕκαστοι τὰ οὐνόματα. τοῦτο καὶ ἐγὼ νέος ἔτι ὢν ἐπετέλεσα, καὶ ἔτι μευ ἐν τῷ ἱρῷ καὶ ὁ πλόκαμος καὶ τὸ οὔνομα.

The young men dedicate the first growth on their chin, then they let down the locks of the maidens, which have been sacred from their birth; they then cut these off [72] in the temple and place them in vessels, some in silver vessels, some in gold, and after placing these in the temple and inscribing the name on the vessel they depart. I performed this act myself when a youth, and my hair remains still in the temple, with my name on the vessel.

---

72. See also § 55, where a first act of the pilgrim is to shave his head; and § 6, where it appears that at Byblos the female locks could be sacrificed as an alternative to offering their own persons. At Trœzene, according to Pausanias (xxxii.), the custom was to sacrifice the hair before marriage. In Catullus, Ode lxvi., Berenice dedicates her hair to Venus. On the general question, see Robertson-Smith, *op. cit.*, p. 329.

APPENDIX.

EXTRACT I.

From *Maundrell's Travels*. Page 153 (6th ed. 1749).
AN ACCOUNT OF THE AUTHOR'S JOURNEY TO THE BANKS OF THE EUPHRATES, ETC., IN HIS "JOURNEY FROM ALEPPO TO JERUSALEM." 1697.

Wednesday, April 19*th.*

WE went east and by north, and in four hours arrived at Bambych. This place has no remnants of its ancient greatness, but its walls, which may be traced all round, and cannot be less than three miles in compass. Several fragments of them remain on the east side, especially at the east gate; and another piece of eighty yards long, with towers of large square stone extremely well built. On the north side I found a stone with the busts of a man and woman, large as life; and under, two Eagles carved on it. Not far from it, on the side of a large well, was fixed a stone with three figures carved on it, in Basso Relievo. They were two Syrens, which twining their fishy tails together, made a seat, on which was placed sitting a naked woman, her arms and the Syrens on each side mutually entwined.

On the west side is a deep pit of about 100 yards diameter. It was low, and had now water in it, and seemed to have had great buildings all round it; with the pillars and ruins of which, it is now in part filled up; but not so much, but that there was still water in it. Here are a multitude of subterraneous aqueducts brought to the city; the people attested no fewer than fifty. You can ride nowhere about the city, without seeing them. We pitched by one about a quarter of a mile east of the city, which yields a fine stream; and emptying itself into a valley, waters it, and makes it extremely fruitful. Here perhaps were the pastures of the beasts designed for sacrifices. Here are now only a few poor inhabitants, tho' anciently all the north side was well inhabited by Saracens;

as may be seen by the remains of a noble Mosque and a Bagnio a little without the walls.

EXTRACT II.
Pocock's Description Of The East. Vol. Ii., Pt. I. (1745); Pp. 166 And 167..

... Bambouch, commonly called by the Franks Bambych, and by the ancients Hierapolis, which was the Greek name that was given it by Seleucus; it was called also Bambyce, which seems to be the Syrian name still retained; and it is very remarkable that Hierapolis in Asia Minor has much the same name, being called Pambouk Calasi (the cotton castle). The Tables make it twenty-four miles distant from Zeuma on the Euphrates and from Ceciliana: They place it also seventy-two miles from Berya, though this is not above fifty from Aleppo. One of the Syrian names of this place was Magog;[1] which was a city of the Cyrrhestica, and is situated at the south end of a long vale, which is about a quarter of a mile broad, watered with a stream that is approached by the aqueducts of Bambych; and, to preserve the water from being wasted, it passes through this vale in an artificial channel or aqueduct which is built of stone on a level with the ground. The form of this site was irregular; some parts of the walls which remain entire, are nine feet thick, and above thirty feet high; they are cased with hewn stone both inside and out, and are about two miles in circumference; there was a walk all round on top of the walls, to which there is an ascent by a flight of stairs, which are built on arches; the wall is defined by towers on five sides, at the distance of fifty paces from each other, and there is a low fosse without the walls. The four gates of the city are about fifteen feet wide, and defended by a semi-circular tower on each side; the water that supplied the town, as I was informed, comes from a hill about twelve miles to the south, and the city being on the advanced ground, the water runs in a channel, which is near twenty feet below the surface of the earth, and in several parts of the city there are holes down to the water about five feet wide,

---

1. Caele habet—Bambycen, quae alio nomine Hierapolis vocatur, Syris vero Magog. Ibi prodigiosa Atargatis, Graecis autem Derceto dicta, colitur. Plin. *Nat. Hist.* V. 19.

Appendix

and fifteen long, with two stones across, one about five feet, the other about ten feet from the top, in order, as may be supposed, to facilitate the descent of the water; it is probable that they had some machines to draw up the water at these holes. In the side of one of them I saw a stone about four feet long, and three wide, on which there was a relief of two winged persons holding a sheet behind a woman a little over her head; they seem to carry her on their fishy tails which join together, and were probably designed to represent the Zephyrs, carrying Venus to the sea.

At the west part of the town there is a dry bason, which seemed to have been triangular; it is close to the town wall; at one corner of it there is a round building which seems to have extended into a bason, and probably was designed in order to behold with greater conveniency some religious ceremonies or public sports. This may be the lake where they had sacred fishes that were tame.

About two hundred paces within the east gate there is a raised ground, on which probably stood a temple of the Syrian goddess Atargatis, thought to be the same as Ashteroth of the Sidonians, and Cybele of the Romans, for whose worship this place was so famous. I conjectured it to be about two hundred feet in front. It is probable that this is the high ground from which they threw people headlong in their religious ceremonies, and sometimes even their own children, though they must inevitably perish. I observed a low wall running from it to the gate, so that probably it had such a grand avenue as the temple at Gerrhae; and the enclosure of the city is irregular in this part, as if some ground had been taken in after the building of the walls to make that grand entrance; it is probable that all the space north of the temple belonged to it. A court is mentioned to the north of the temple, and a tower likewise before the temple, which was built on a terrace twelve feet high. If this tower was on the high ground I mentioned, the temple must have been west of it, of which I could see no remains; it possibly might have been where there are now some ruins of a large building, which seems to have been a church with a tower; to the west of which there are some ruinous arches, which might be part of a portico. It is said that not only Syria, Cilicia, and Cappadocia, contributed to the support of this

temple, but even Arabia, and the territories of Babylon: To the west of the town there is a high ground, and some burial places; and so there are also to the north-east, where I saw inscriptions in the oriental languages, and several crosses. At a little distance from the north-east corner of the town there is a building like a church, but within it there is some Gothic work, such as is seen in antient mosques; and there is a room on each side of the south end; the whole is ruinous, but very strongly built, and they call it the house of Phila.

EXTRACT III.
The Expedition To The Euphrates And Tigris.
By Colonel Chesney. London, 1850. Vol. I., Ch. XVIII., pp. 420 and 421.

. . . .

[Nine miles below the mouth of the Sajur, the fine Saracenic structure of Kal-at-en-Nejm commands the remains of the great Zeugma leading to Seroug, Haran, etc., and 11 miles directly south by west from thence on four hills, are the extensive remains of the castle and town of Kara Bambuche, or Buyuk Munbedj,[2] which contains some fine excavations near the river, and also a Zeugma, but in a more dilapidated state, being without the slopes which, when passing at Kal-at-en-Nejm, served for landing places at different heights of the river.]

Sixteen miles west by south of the latter, and 11½ miles south-west of the former passage, at about 600 feet above the river Euphrates, the ruins of the Magog of the Syrians occupy the centre of a rocky plain, where, by its isolated position, the city must not only have been deprived of running water, but likewise of every other advantage which was likely to create and preserve a place of importance. Yet we know that the Syrian city of Ninus Vetus [3] flourished under the name of Bambyce[4] and subsequently

---

2. Jisr Munbedj, two days from Haran. Jaubert's *Edrisi*, p. 155, tome VI.; *Recueil de Voyages*, etc. Paris, 1840.

3. Ammian. *Mar.*, XIV., c. viii.

4. The Syrian name of the city, which the Greeks afterwards called Hierapolis. Strabo, XVI., p. 747.

of Hierapolis,[5] or the Sacred City of the Greeks,[6] and that it contained the rich temple which was plundered by Crassus;[7] finally it bore the name of Munbedj[8] or Bambuche, and had a succession of sovereigns in the 5th century of the Hijrah.[9] The ancient city was near the eastern extremity of Commagene, or Euphratensis, which had Samosat at the opposite extremity.[10]

Some ruined mosques and square Saracenic towers, with the remains of its surrounding walls and ditch, marked the limits of the Muslim city; within which are four large cisterns, a fine sarcophagus, and, among other ancient remains the sculptured ruins of an acropolis, and those of two temples. Of the smaller, the enclosure and portions of seven columns remain; but it seems to possess little interest compared with the larger, which may have been that of the Assyrian and Phœnician Astarte,[11] or Astroarche (queen of stars), which afterwards became the Syrian Atargatis,[12] or Venus Decerto.[13] Amongst the remains of the latter are some fragments of massive architecture, not unlike the Egyptian, and 11 arches from one side of a square paved court, over which are scattered the shafts of columns and capitals displaying the lotus.

A little way westward of the walls there is an extensive necropolis, which contains many Turkish, with some Pagan, Seljukian, and Syriac tombs; the last having some almost illegible inscriptions in the ancient character.

---

5. Ammian. *Mar.*, XIV., c. viii.
6. Hierapolis, or Magog, in Syriac. Plin. lib. V., c. xxiii.
7. Plutarch in Crassus.
8. It was first built by the Persians, who had a fine temple there. Muhammed Ibn Sepahi's *Clear Knowledge of Cities and Kingdoms.*
9. Des Guignes, *His. des Huns*, tome II., p. 275.
10. Amm. *Mar.* XIV., c. viii.
11. There were temples of this goddess in Palestine. Jos. Ant., lib. V., c. xiv. 8; at Tyre, *ibid.*; against Apion, lib. I., s. 19; and at Sidon, 1. Kings, c. v., and v. 33.
12. Strabo, XVI., p. 748.
13. Herod., lib. I., c. cv., mentions the temple of Venus at Askalon, which, in Diod. *Sic.*, lib. II., is called that of Decerto. There was another temple of Venus, or Atargatis, at Joppa. Plin., lib. V., c. xiii. and xxiii.

BIBLIOGRAPHY

[We have to thank Dr. Barnett, of the British Museum, for his courtesy in presenting us with the Bibliography of the translations and editions of Lucian.]

GREEK AND LATIN

Luciani omnia quae extant, cum latina interpretatione (of J. Micyllus, M. Bolerus, D. Erasmus, etc.). Paris, 1615. Fol.

Luciani opera omnia, J. Benedictus emendavit. Salmurii, 1619. 8vo.

Luciani Samosatensis opera, ex versione J. Benedicti. Cum notis J. Bourdelotii, etc. Amstelodami, 1687. 8vo.

Luciani opera, cum nova versione T. Hemsterhusii et J. M. Gesneri, etc. Amstelodami, Trajecti ad Rhenum, 1743-6. 4to.

Luciani opera, cum notis selectis. Curavit J. P. Schmidius. Leipzig, 1776-80. 8vo.

Luciani opera ad editionem T. Hemsterhusii et J. F. Reitzii accurate expressa cum annotationibus. Biponti, 1789-93. 8vo.

Luciani opera, castigata, edidit J. T. Lehmann. Lipsiae, 1822-31. 8vo.

Luciani opera ex recensione G. Dindorfii. Parisiis, 1840. 8vo.

Luciani opera ex recensione G. Dindorfii. Editio altera emendators. Parisiis, 1867. 8vo.

LATIN

Luciani opera, in latinum, partim diversis autoribus, partim per J. Micyllum, translata. Francofurti, 1543. Fol.

ENGLISH

Lucian's works, translated from the Greek. By F. Spence. London, 1684-5. 8vo.

The works of Lucian, translated from the Greek, by several eminent hands (T. Ferne, W. Moyle, Sir H. Sheere, A. Baden, C. Blount, T. Brown, J. Drake, S. Cobb, Gildon, Cashen, Vernon, Sprag, Hill, S. Atkinson, H. Blount, Ayloffe, J. Philips, L. Eachard, C. Eachard, Savage, J. Digby, H. Hare, J. Washington, N. Tate, and Sir J. Tyrell). With the life of Lucian, a discourse on his writings, and a character of some of the present translators, by J. Dryden. London, 1711. 8vo.

The works of Lucian, from the Greek, by T. Francklin. London, 1780. 4to.

Lucian, from the Greek, with the comments and illustrations of Wieland and others. By W. Tooke. London, 1820. 4to.

The Works of Lucian of Samosata. Translated by H. W. Fowler and F. G. Fowler. Oxford, 1905.

FRENCH

Les oeuvres de Lucien, traduites du grec, par F. Bretin. Paris, 1583. Fol.

Lucian, de la traduction de N. Perrot, Sr. d'Ablancourt. Paris, 1654. 4to.

Lucian, de la traduction de N. Perrot, Sr. d'Ablancourt. Paris, 1674. 8vo.

Lucian, de la traduction de N. Perrot, Sr. d'Ablancourt. Amsterdam, 1709. 8vo.

Oeuvres de Lucian, traduites du grec, avec des remarques, sur le texte, et la collation de six manuscrits de la Bibliothèque du Roi (by J. N. Belin de Ballu). Paris, 1789. 8vo.

Oeuvres complètes. Traduction de Belin de Ballu, revue corrigée et complétée, par Louis Humbert. Paris, 1896.

GERMAN

Lucians von Samosata sämtliche Werke. Aus dem Griechischen übersetzt und mit Anmerkungen versehen von C. M. Wieland. Leipzig, 1788-9. 8vo.

ITALIAN

Le opere di Luciano, volgarizzate da G. Manzi. Losanna, 1819. 8vo.

SPANISH

Obras completas, traducidas, por D. C. Vidal y F. Delgado. Madrid, 1882, etc. 8vo.

GREEK AND ENGLISH

Lucian. Literally and completely translated, from the Greek text of C. Jacobitz. (Athenian Society's Publications). London, 1895.

INDEX

A

ABD-HADAD, Priest-King of Hierapolis, 21
Achilles, effigy of, 79
'Adad (see also Hadad), name of the god of Hierapolis, 19
Adargatis, name of the goddess according to Macrobius, 19
Adonis, myth of, 3; river, 41; sacrifice to, 39; wounded, the legend of, 41
Agdistis, goddess of the Phrygians, 1
Agenor, 37
Agriculture, Hittite god of, 7
Aleppo, bronze figure of goddess from, 12
Alexandria, Lucian at, 24; statue of, 81; the false prophet, 24
Altar, draped, 10; of brass, 79; pedestal, draped, 18, 74
Andromache, effigy of, 79
Animals, sacred, 81
Antioch, Lucian at, 23
Aphaca, temple of Aphrodite at, 43
Aphrodite, sacrifice to, 39; Syrian goddess embodies attributes of, 71; temple of, at Aphaca, 43
Apollo, a bearded, 75; oriental aspects of, 75
Archives of the Hittites, 4
Arms, the Hittite god of, 5
Artemis, Syrian goddess embodies attributes of, 71
Ashtoreth, 37; the goddess, 1
Asia Minor, attributes of the goddess in, 2
Askalon, connection with Atargatis, 20
Assemblies, sacred, 85
Assyria, used for Syria, 35
Astarte, as a Hittite goddess, 1; of Phœnicia, 1, 12; the Phœnician, 37
Atargatis, 34; goddess of Hierapolis, 1 (see also Goddess); identified with Derceto, 47; resemblance to Kybele, 49; son of, 6; spelling and composition of the name, 16; the priest of, 20

'Athar, name of Ishtar in Syria, 1
Atheh, goddess of Cilicia, 47; name of Cilician goddess, 1
Athene, Syrian goddess embodies attributes of, 71
Atlas, statue of, 79
Attes, traditional founder of the shrine at Hierapolis, 49
Attis, in legend and religion, 3; priest, possibly represented in Hittite art, 8
Axe, the double, emblem of Bellona, 14; the, emblem of thunder, 4

B

BAAL, of Tarsus, 36; Kevan, suggested name of the god, 17
Bambyce, earliest name of Hierapolis, 34
Bellona, Roman goddess, identified with goddess of Comana, 13
Bird, consecration of, 25; in Hittite art, 11; symbol of the goddess, 10
Birth, goddess of, 12
Boar, wild, legend of, 39
Boghaz-Keui, Hittite god and goddess at, 5; sanctuary of youthful deity, 6
Bow, borne by Hittite deity, 5; in Hittite art, 11
Brazen statue at Hierapolis, 65
Bull, as counterpart of goddess on coins, 14; Europa sitting upon, 37; god, the Hittite, 8; Hadad leading a, 5; Hittite deity identified with, 5; replaces god in art, 8
Bulls, god seated on, 71
Byblos, Aphrodite of, 39; legend of Osiris at, 41; temple at, 39

C

CAPITAL, the, of the Hittites, 3
Carchemish, fall of, 13; sculpture from, 6; sculptures of the goddess at, 11
Castration, 3, 51, 65
Caves, the goddess of, 6
Child, on knee of goddess, in Hittite art, 11 Christianity, in the time of Lucian, 27
Coast of Asia Minor, Hittites advance towards the, 4
Cock (sacred), 85
Coins of Hierapolis, 15
Comana, the goddess of war at, 13
Combabus, legends of, 57; statue of, 81
Commagene, 35

Communion scene in Hittite art, 10
Cones, sacred, of the goddess, 67
Conical obelisk, 38
Constantine destroys the shrine at Aphaca, 42
Corpses, unlucky to see, 87
Crœsus, of Lydia, 13

D

DEA SYRIA, the local goddess of Hierapolis, identified with Atargatis, *q.v.* (see Goddess), 16; seated and robed, 16
Dead, the goddess of the, 11
Deluge, legend of, 45
Derceto, image of, 49; in form of a fish, 49; the fish goddess, 47
Deukalion, the story of, 45
Dionysus, 75; assumes woman's dress, 50; legendary founder of the temple at Hierapolis, 51
Distaff, carried by the Syrian goddess, 71
Divination, 77
Divine, father and mother, 6; marriage, 6; Triad, 7
Dodona, Zeus of, 6
Doliche, survival of Hittite cult at, 13
Dove, in Hittite art, 19; symbol of goddess, 17; the, 74
Doves, in Babylonian art, 88
Draped, altar, 10; altar pedestal, 74
Drum, carried by Atargatis, 51
Dual cult, at Hierapolis, 9; of Hittite origins, 8; substantiated on coins, 19

E

EAGLE, double-headed, 8; temple of the, 79; triumphing over lion on coins, 17
Earth, the fruits of, personified, 7
Earth-goddess in Greece, 6
Earth-Mother (see Earth-goddess), 6
Effigies of "Zeus" and "Hera" at Hierapolis, 71
Effigy of Apollo, bearded, 75; of fish-goddess, 49
Egyptian temples, 35
Eilithyia, statue of, 79

Empire, extent of Hittite, 4
Europa, 37
Exogamy, 39
Eyuk, double-headed eagle at, 8; goddess worshipped at, 11; Hittite sculptures at, 8

F

FASSILER, Hittite monument at, 67
Fates, the, Syrian goddess embodies attributes of, 71
Feast, the ceremonial feast in Hittite sculptures, 11; the Ceremonial, 10
Festival of the Pyre, 85
Fish goddess, 49
Fishes, holy, 49
Flood, the, legend of, 25, 45
Fraktin, Hittite sculptures of, 74; Hittite sculptures at, 10

G

GALLI, the, 14, 61, 81, 87; customs of the, 65
Garments on trees, 85
Girdle, the, 71
Goats sacrificed to Hittite god, 8
God of Hierapolis, identical with Hittite chief deity, 9; on coins, 17
God on bull throne, 17
God, the chief Hittite, 4; resembles Zeus, 5; dominant, 8; fall of, 13
God, the youthful Hittite, 6
Goddess of Hierapolis, identified, 9; described by Lucian, 9; recognizable, 15; seated on lion, 16
" on lion throne, 17; two varieties of, 11; of War at Comana, identified with Bellona, 14
" the chief Hittite, resembles the Great Mother, 6; the leading Hittite, 1
" the Hittite, seated, 8; seated and robed, 12; wedded, 15
" the Mother, survival of cult, 14; as goddess of the dead, 11
" the Nature, explanation of abnormal tendencies, 3; in Asia Minor, 2; in Babylonia, 1; worship long established in Asia Minor, 4
Gods, the minor Hittite, 6
Great Mother, the (see Goddess)

H

HADAD, name of Syrian deity, 4; of Hierapolis, 8; statue of, carried, 77

Hadad-Zeus, term describing the Hittite deity, 9

Hair, dedicated, 93; locks of, consecrated, 25

Hammer, emblem of thunder, 4

Heaven, Lord of, title of Hittite god, 4

Hecuba, effigy of, 79

Helen, effigy of, 79

Heliopolitan Triad, 20

Hera, goddess of Hierapolis called, 71; name given by Lucian to the goddess of Hierapolis, 9; offerings, 39; previously married, 6; Sancta, consort of Jupiter Dolichenus, 13; seen in a vision by Stratonice, 55; the Assyrian, 35

Hercules, of Tyre, 37; assumes woman's dress, 50

Hermes, statue of, 79

Hermocles, statue ascribed to, 65

Hierapolis, 35; bull-god on coins of, 8; central cult of Hittite origins, 9; coins of Atargatis at, 12; images in the sanctuary of, 9; name of the goddess at, 1; site of, 34; the shrine at, 43

Hierapolitan Triad, 20

High-priest, 81; the Hittite, 8

Hippolytus, 61

Hittite, Chief Deity, 4; goddess, 1; dress, survival on coin, 20

Hittites, the, in history, 4; end of their domination, 12

I

IMAGE, of the god carried, 6, 77; of the Mother-goddess, 10

Images, votive, of the naked goddess, 11

Ionic dialect, 24, 25

Ishtar, the goddess, 1; as goddess of the dead, 11; among the Mitanni, 8

Ivriz, Hittite sculpture at, 7, 36, 77

J

JUPITER Dolichenus, 13

K

KARA-BURSHLU, sculptures of the Hittite goddess at, 10
King-Priest, the Hittite, 8
Kizil-Dagh, Hittite deity carved on, 6
Kubile (Kybele) in Phrygian art, 11
Kybele (or Rhea), resemblance to goddess of Hierapolis, 19; in the West, 71; and Attis, cult of, 14; legends of, at Hierapolis, 49; Attis as a son of, 3

L

LAKE, sacred, at Hierapolis, 80
Libation, 81; in Hittite worship, 91
Lion, devouring bull, on coins, 16; emblematic of earth, 19; goddess seated on, 16; throne, on coins, 16
Lioness, goddess on, 8
Lions, draw effigy of Atargatis, 51; goddess seated on, 71
Lituus, emblem of Hittite priesthood, 8
Lord of Heaven, title of Hittite god, 4
Loss of Hierapolis, 34
Lucian returns to Samosata, 24
Lyre, in Hittite art, 11

M

MA, goddess of Comana, 1
Mabog, Syrian name of Hierapolis, 35
Macrobius, describes the cult of the Syrian goddess, 15; describes the Syrian god and goddess, 19; quoted, 75
Malâtia, Hittite sculptures at, 4; local deity of, identified, 7
Mannikins of wood, 53, 67
Marash, sculptures of the Hittite goddess at, 11
Marriage scene at Boghaz-Keui, 6
Mated divinities in Cilicia and Phœnicia, 14
Mermaid, effigy like a, 48
Mirror in Hittite art, 11
Mitanni, treaty of Hittites with, 8

Mother-earth (see Earth-goddess).
"   -goddess (see Goddess).
"   of the gods, 19
Mount Lebanus, 41
Mumbidj, identified with Hierapolis, 34
Musicians, 81
Mylitta, name of Ishtar in Herodotus, 12
Myth of Ishtar and Tammuz, 2

N

NAKED goddess, 12
Nanai, goddess of Pre-semitic Babylonia, 1
Nature-goddess (see Goddess of Nature).
Nemesis, Syrian goddess embodies attributes of, 71
Nigrinus, the philosopher, 23
Nireus, statue of, 79

O

OBLATION scene in Hittite art, 10
Oracles, 77; at Hierapolis, 43
Osiris, legend of, at Byblos, 41

P

PAPHOS, pillars at, 67
Paris, effigy of, 79
Peregrinus, the impostor, 24
Phalli, ascent of the, 67; dedicated by Dionysus, 51
Philomela, statue of, 79
Phrygian goddess, 19
Phrygians in Asia Minor, 13
Pigeon, a golden, 75; emblem of Semiramis, 49
Pilgrimages to Hierapolis, 43
Pillar of altar, draped, 18

Pillars, pairs of, 66
Poem by Catullus, 3
Priestess, the high, 8
Priestesses, Hittite representations of, 8
Priesthood of Attis, 3
Priest-King, the Hittite, 8
Priests, 81; of the goddess, 14
Procne, statue of, 79
Prostitution, sacred, 14, 39
Pteria, fall of, 13

R

RAMMAN, incorrect rendering of name 'Adad, 4
Rams, sacrificed to Hittite god, 8
Red colour of Adonis River, 41
Religion in the East, 14
Rhea (or Kybele), resemblance to goddess of Hierapolis, 19; legends of, 49; Syrian goddess embodies attributes of, 71
Robed goddess, 11
Rome, Lucian at, 24

S

SACRIFICES, 83
Sakje-Geuzi, goddess worshipped at, 11; Hittite walls at, 66
Sammuramat, identified with Semiramis, 47
Samosata, birthplace of Lucian, 23
Samsat, birthplace of Lucian, 35; Hittite remains at, 35
Sanctuary of Hierapolis, described, 71; represented on coin, 17
Sandan, possible effigy of, at Hierapolis, 77
Sandan-Hercules of Ivriz, 20
Sardanapalus, statue of, 81
Sceptre, carried by the Syrian goddess, 71
Selene, Syrian goddess embodies attributes of, 71
Semiramis, 49, 75; effigy of, 75; image of, 79
Senjerli, Hittite storm god at, 4; the Syro-Hittite city at, 66
Shaving of heads, 39
Shepherd origin of Attis, 3

Shrines, Græco-Phœnician, 38
Simios, lover of Atargatis, 20
Sipylus, Mount, image of the goddess on, 10
Solomon, temple of, at Jerusalem, 66
Son of Atargatis, 20
Statue, brazen, at Hierapolis, 65; of the goddess carried, 77
Statues, of the god and goddess of Hierapolis, 71; of gods, moved, at Hierapolis, 43
Stheneboea, 61
Storms, controller of, attribute of Hittite god, 4
Stratonice, legendary builder of temple at Hierapolis, 53
Subject-matter of the «De Dea Syria,» 31
Suidas› life of Lucian, 23
Sun, Hittite god identified with, 4
Sun-god, a throne for the, 75
Survival of Hittite dress at Hierapolis, 21; of cult, 15
Swine, abhorrence of, 89; god, 89
Syria, coalition of the Hittites in, 12
Syrian cults impassioned, 12
Syro-Cappodocians, 13

T

TAMMUZ, relation to Ishtar, 2
Tarsus, bull-god on coins of, 8
Tattooing, 91
Taurus Region, submission of, 13
Temple at Hierapolis, described, 69; its sizes, 67; legends about the, 59; position of the, 67
Temples in Syria, 35
Teshub, identical with chief Hittite deity, 4
Text of the "De Dea Syria," 28
Thor's hammer, 4
Tower, head-dress of Atargatis, 51
Treaty with Egypt, 1
Triad, of Hierapolis, 20; the divine, 7
Tyre, Hercules of, 37

U

UNION of two deities, 6

V

VEDIC deities, 50
Vegetation, the god of, 77

W

WALLS, double, in North Syria, 67
Water, brought to the temple, 47
Wedded deities at Hierapolis, 9
Winged deity from Carchemish, 12
Woman in service of the goddess, 14
Woman›s dress, Attes in, 51
Women in Hittite art, 83; in the temple service, 81
Women›s dress, men assume, 65

X

XANTHOS, legend of Atargatis and her son, 20
Xisuthros, story of the flood, 44

Y

YAHWEH, resemblance of Hittite deity to, 4
Yarre in Phrygia, image of the goddess at, 10

Z

ZEUS and Europa, 37; as a god of agriculture, etc., in Greece, 8; as a bull-god, 37; god of Hierapolis called, 71; Hagios, 13; the Dodonian, 6; the name given by Lucian to the god of Hierapolis, 9
Zeus-Hadad, term describing the Hittite deity, 9

www.ingramcontent.com/pod-product-compliance
Lightning Source LLC
Chambersburg PA
CBHW071708040426
42446CB00011B/1969